Titel/Title

www.ebn24.com

Wirtschafts- und Wissenschaftsstandort Region Dresden
Business and Science Location of the Dresden Region

Chancen und Perspektiven einer Region
Opportunities and Prospects of a Region

EUROPÄISCHER WIRTSCHAFTS VERLAG
Region Dresden
2009/2010

Vorwort/Foreword

Christian Kirk

Vorstandsvorsitzender der MEDIEN GRUPPE KIRK AG
CEO of MEDIEN GRUPPE KIRK AG

Sehr geehrte Damen und Herren,

Dresden ist in den letzten Jahren in die Top 20 der deutschen Wirtschaftsstandorte aufgestiegen. In Ostdeutschland liegt die Landeshauptstadt laut Zukunftsatlas 2007 sogar auf Platz 1. Grund für diesen rasanten Aufstieg ist unter anderem das außerordentlich hohe Bildungsniveau. Rund 20 Prozent der Beschäftigten haben einen Hochschulabschluss. Die Forschungsergebnisse der mehr als 120 Institute sorgen weltweit für Aufsehen und Anerkennung. Dies ist die Basis für den Hightech-Standort Dresden. Allein in der Mikroelektronik sowie Informations- und Kommunikationstechnologie sind über 20.000 Beschäftigte tätig. Der Wirtschafts- und Wissenschaftsstandort Dresden bietet darüber hinaus, mit Semperoper oder der Gemäldegalerie, ein umfassendes Angebot an Kunst und Kultur. Den Namen „Elbflorenz" verdankt die Stadt ihrer ausgeprägten Barockarchitektur, die auch die Frauenkirche, eine der bekanntesten Kirchen der Welt, prägt. Das nahegelegene Elbsandsteingebirge lädt zudem zum Wandern und Klettern ein.

Dieses Buch soll Kooperationen und neue Geschäftskontakte mit den hier präsentierten Unternehmen und Ihnen als Lesern fördern. Es ist wichtiger Bestandteil des Standardwerkes zu europäischen Wirtschaftsregionen und international auch im Internet unter www.ebn24.com präsent.

Dear Reader,

Dresden has, over the past years, ascended to one of the top 20 German business locations. According to the Zukunftsatlas 2007, the state capital actually lies in first place in Eastern Germany. The cause for this rapid ascent is, amongst others, the extraordinarily high level of education. Around 20 per cent of employed people are in possession of a university degree. The research results of more than 120 research institutes cause world wide sensations and enjoy high reputation. This is the foundation of the Dresden high-tech location. The microelectronics industry alone, as well as the information and communication technology industry, employ more than 20,000 people. The Dresden economic and scientific location furthermore offers a comprehensive selection of art and culture, featuring the Semper Opera or the Gemäldegalerie. The city owes the name "Elbflorence" to its distinct Baroque architecture, also characteristic of the Frauenkirche, which is one of the most renowned churches in the world. Moreover, the nearby Elbe Sandstone Mountains invite one for hiking and rock climbing.

This book aims to promote cooperation and new business contacts between the herein represented companies and you as the reader. It is an important part of the standard works on European economic regions and can also be accessed internationally at www.ebn24.com.

Vorwort/Foreword

Stanislaw Tillich

Ministerpräsident des Freistaates Sachsen
Minister President of the Free State of Saxony

Sehr geehrte Damen und Herren,

der Wirtschafts- und Wissenschaftsstandort rund um die Landeshauptstadt Dresden ist schon hinsichtlich Dichte an Forschungs-Instituten der Fraunhofer- und der Max-Planck-Gesellschaft bundesweit herausragend. Ein Umfeld, in dem auch führende Unternehmen angesiedelt sind, die in verschiedenen Bereichen der Zukunftstechnologien Innovationen entwickeln und dabei täglich Wettbewerbsfähigkeit demonstrieren. Die auch durch die Verbundinitiativen geförderte Innovationskraft der Unternehmen und wissenschaftlichen Einrichtungen in der Region Dresden wirkt sich dabei fruchtbar auf das ganze Land und den Standort Deutschland aus. Dies unterstützt die Landesregierung: Seit 1991 haben wir mehr als 1,3 Milliarden Euro als Zuschüsse für betriebliche Technologieprojekte investiert. Die Region beweist: Wissenschaft und Technologie sind der Motor des Fortschritts. Wir können dabei stolz darauf sein, dass aufgrund der gezielten Ansiedlungspolitik Hightech-Unternehmen sowohl in den großen Städten wie im ländlichen Raum beheimatet sind. Damit das so bleibt, setzt die Landesregierung neben dem Ausbau des Bildungssektors einen besonderen Schwerpunkt ihrer Mittelstandspolitik auf Forschung und Entwicklung in den KMU, denn gerade sie sind die wesentlichen Eckpfeiler für Wachstum und Beschäftigung.

Dear Reader,

The business and scientific location around the state capital of Dresden is prominent nationwide as regards the concentration of research institutions of the Fraunhofer and Max Planck societies. An environment in which also leading organizations are resident, which develop future technological innovations in numerous fields and in doing so, demonstrate competitiveness on a daily basis. Besides, the innovative strength also promoted by the network initiatives of enterprises and scientific facilitys in the Dresden region affects the whole land and the location of Germany in a fertile way. This is supported by the state government: Since 1991, we have invested more than 1.3 billion euros as subsidies for operational technology projects. The region demonstrates: Science and technology are the driving forces for progress. We can therefore be proud that, due to settlement policies targeting high-tech organizations, both the large cities as the rural region are well-established. In order for this to persist, the state government, in addition to the upgrading of the educational sector, places a particular focus on its small-firm business policies in research and development in the small and medium-sized business sector, since precisely they are the essential cornerstones for growth and employment.

Wirtschafts- und Wissenschaftsstandort Region Dresden
Business and Science Location of the Dresden Region

Christian Kirk Vorstandsvorsitzender der Medien Gruppe Kirk AG	Vorwort Foreword	3
Stanislaw Tillich Ministerpräsident des Freistaates Sachsen	Vorwort Foreword	5
Thomas Jurk Sächsischer Staatsminister für Wirtschaft und Arbeit und Stellvertretender Ministerpräsident	Wo Wirtschaft auf Wissenschaft trifft Where economy meets science	8
Dr. habil. Henry Hasenpflug Präsident der Landesdirektion Dresden	Die Region Dresden baut aus The Dresden region is developing	12
Dr. Michael Hupe Geschäftsführer der Flughafen Dresden GmbH	Drehscheibe und wichtigste Verkehrsinfrastruktur für die Region A hub and an important transportation infrastructure for the region	20
Dr. Detlef Hamann Hauptgeschäftsführer der Industrie- und Handelskammer Dresden	Hohes Niveau an wirtschaftlichen Verflechtungen im Dreiländereck High level of economic integration at the border triangle	28
Klaus Wurpts Geschäftsführer der Wirtschaftsinitiative für Mitteldeutschland GmbH	Dresden, Sachsen, Mitteldeutschland – Regionale Kooperation als Wettbewerbsvorteil Dresden, Saxony, Middle Germany – Regional cooperation as competitive advantage	34
Dr. Eva-Maria Stange Staatsministerin für Wissenschaft und Kunst des Freistaates Sachsen	Dresden bietet exzellente Forschung und beste Hochschulausbildung Dresden offers excellent research and first-rate tertiary education	40
Ulrich Assmann Vorstandsvorsitzender der TU Dresden AG	Know-how-Transfer in Dresden – Wissen vermarkten, Zukunft gestalten Know-how transfer in Dresden – Promoting knowledge, shaping the future	44
Prof. Dr. Eckhard Beyer Leiter des Fraunhofer-Instituts für Werkstoff- und Strahltechnik	Anwendungsorientierte Forschung für die Unternehmen in der Region Application-oriented research for organizations in the region	50

Contents

Prof. Dr. Kai Simons Vorstandsvorsitzender des BioDresden eV	BIOPOLIS Dresden – Eine Vision wird Wirklichkeit BIOPOLIS Dresden – A vision becomes reality	58
Prof. Dr. Peter Kücher Institutsleiter, Fraunhofer Center Nanoelektronische Technologien	Nanoelektronik – Praxisnahe Forschung in neuen Kooperationsformen Nanoelectronics – Practical research in new cooperation models	66
Andreas Huhn Präsident, Sachsenmetall Unternehmensverband der Elektroindustrie eV	Hier stimmt die Mischung – Ideale Verhältnisse für Metall und Elektro Here the mixture is right – Ideal conditions for metal and electrics	74
Prof. Dr.-Ing. Dieter Weidlich Projektmanager der Verbundinitiative Maschinenbau Sachsen VEMAS	Region für die Zukunft gut gerüstet A region well-equipped for the future	78
Markus H. Michalow Mitglied der Geschäftsführung, Dresdner Bank AG, Dresden	Mezzaninkapital – Innovative Finanzierungsmethoden für den Mittelstand Mezzanine capital – Innovative financing methods for medium-sized businesses	84
Dr. Wilhelm W. Zörgiebel Geschäftsführer der Grundbesitz Hellerau GmbH	Tradition und Moderne – Technologiezentren im Innovationswettbewerb Traditional and modern spirits – Technology centres in innovative competition	90
Gerhard Riegger Direktor der MARITIM Hotelgesellschaft Dresden	Dresden erlangt Topposition in der Kongress- und Tagungsbranche Dresden gained top position in the congress and conference business	98
Prof. Gerd Uecker Intendant der Sächsischen Staatsoper Dresden	Die Semperoper – Ein Leuchtturm in der Dresdner Kulturlandschaft The Semper Opera House – A beacon in the Dresden cultural landscape	104
Hauke Haensel Präsident der SG Dynamo Dresden eV	Bessere Bedingungen für attraktiven Sport – Dresden bekommt ein neues Stadion Better conditions for attractive sport – Dresden gets a new stadium	110
	Standort auf einen Blick The location at a glance	116
	Verzeichnis der vorgestellten Unternehmen List of companies	118
	Impressum Imprint	120

Wo Wirtschaft auf Wissenschaft trifft
Where economy meets science

Thomas Jurk

Der Autor, 1962 in Görlitz geboren, arbeitete nach seiner Ausbildung zum Funkmechaniker bis 1989 bei der PGH Elektro, Rundfunk, Fernsehen Weißwasser. Seit 1990 ist er Mitglied im sächsischen Landtag. Ab 1999 führte er die SPD-Fraktion an. Seit 2004 ist Thomas Jurk stellvertretender Ministerpräsident und sächsischer Staatsminister für Wirtschaft und Arbeit.

The author was born in Görlitz in 1962. After an apprenticeship as a radio technician, he worked at PGH Elektro, Rundfunk, Fernsehen Weißwasser until 1989. He has been a member of Saxony's State Legislature since 1990. From 1999, he was the leader of the SPD faction in the State Legislature. He has been Deputy Prime Minister and State Minister for Economic Affairs and Labour since 2004.

Die Region Dresden gehört ohne Zweifel zu den zukunftsorientierten Wirtschaftsstandorten. Hohe Lebensqualität und gute Investitionsbedingungen haben der Region international einen guten Ruf beschert. Viele Mittelständler haben ihr Unternehmen in erfolgreiche Bahnen gelenkt; viele große Unternehmen haben den Weg nach Dresden gefunden. Ob Maschinenbauer, anspruchsvoller Ingenieurdienstleister oder Hersteller von Infrarot-Kabinen für medizinische Anwendungen: Die Liste der Neuansiedlungen zeigt ein breites Spektrum.

Die Erfahrungen mit dem wirtschaftlichen Umbruch 1989 haben gezeigt, dass der Erhalt industrieller Kerne und Kompetenzen entscheidend für die Perspektiven einer Region ist. In Zeiten von Globalisierung und weltweitem Standortwettbewerb wird es zukünftig aber noch mehr darauf ankommen, die Einzigartigkeit der Dresdener Forschungs- und Technologiekonstellation zu vermarkten.

Gerade in einer zunehmend wissensbasierten Wirtschaft werden Innovationen zu einer entscheidenden Größe für Wachstum und Beschäftigung. Nur wenn Forschung und Entwicklung genügend Fachkräfte mit einem hohen Bildungsniveau vorfinden, kann die Region als Ganzes profitieren.

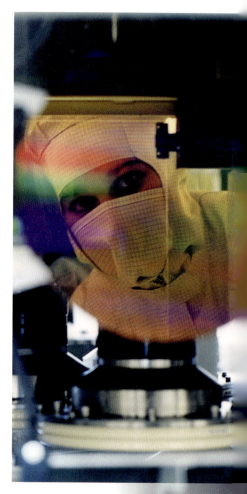

Dresden weist ein Höchstmaß an Forschungsintensität auf.
Dresden exhibits the highest standard of research intensity.

Introduction

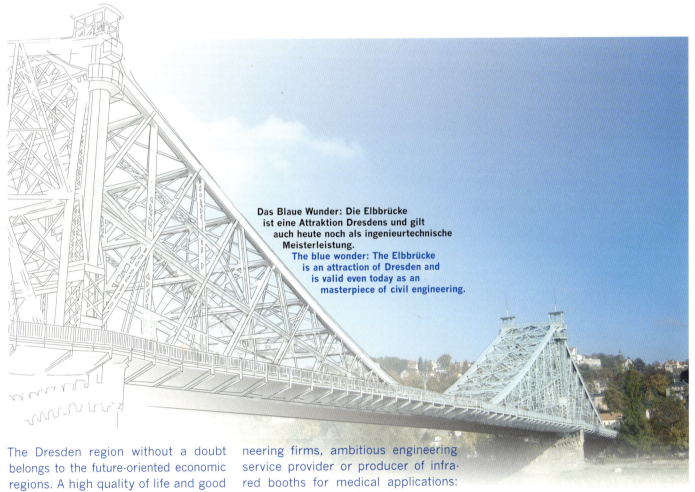

Das Blaue Wunder: Die Elbbrücke ist eine Attraktion Dresdens und gilt auch heute noch als ingenieurtechnische Meisterleistung.
The blue wonder: The Elbbrücke is an attraction of Dresden and is valid even today as an masterpiece of civil engineering.

The Dresden region without a doubt belongs to the future-oriented economic regions. A high quality of life and good investment conditions have brought the region a good reputation internationally. Many entrepreneurs of medium-sized organizations have steered their businesses along successful paths; many large organizations have found their way to Dresden. Be it mechanical engineering firms, ambitious engineering service provider or producer of infrared booths for medical applications: The list of new settlements reveals a wide spectrum.

Experiences with the economic upheaval of 1989 have shown that the preservation of industrial cores and competencies are decisive for the future prospects of a region. In times of globalization and worldwide location competition, the uniqueness of the marketing of the Dresden research and technology constellation will, however, matter even more in the future.

Einleitung

Symbol des Wiederaufbaus:
Die Frauenkirche prägt das Dresdener Stadtbild.
Symbol of reconstruction:
The Frauenkirche shapes the cityscape of Dresden.

Eine enge Verzahnung von Wirtschaft und Wissenschaft ist deshalb eine wichtige Voraussetzung für einen erfolgreichen Innovationsprozess. Mit seinen gut ausgebildeten und hoch motivierten Fachkräften bietet der Wirtschafts- und Wissensstandort Dresden ein besonderes Potenzial, um von dem Transfer wissenschaftlicher und technischer Innovationen in die wirtschaftliche Anwendung zu profitieren.

Um die Verzahnung von Wissenschaft und Wirtschaft weiter auszubauen, hat die sächsische Staatsregierung die Weichen noch stärker auf „Vorrang für Innovation, Wachstum und Beschäftigung" gestellt. Mit zahlreichen förderpolitischen Instrumenten trägt sie zu optimalen Rahmenbedingungen bei, gibt Anreize und Unterstützung.
In der Region Dresden haben Ideenreichtum, Mut und Unternehmergeist Tradition.

Überzeugen Sie sich selbst von den Vorteilen der Region Dresden. Ich bin sicher, wir dürfen uns auch künftig über die wirtschaftlichen und technologischen Erfolge in Dresden und Sachsen freuen.

Introduction

Optimale Infrastruktur an einem Standort, an dem viel bewegt wird.
Optimal infrastructure at a location where there is a lot of movement.

Especially in an increasingly knowledge-based economy, innovations become an important factor for growth and employment.
Only if research and development are able to find sufficient qualified employees with a high level of education, will the region profit in its entirety.

A close interlinking of economics and science is therefore an important prerequisite for a successful innovation process. With its well-educated and highly motivated qualified employees, the Dresden economic and scientific location offers a special potential to profit from the transfer of scientific and technological innovations into commercial application.
In order to further develop the interlinking of science and economy, the Saxon state government has raise the bar high-

er even stronger on "priority for innovation, growth and employment". With numerous political grant instruments, it contributes towards optimal basic conditions, provides incentives and support.
In the Dresden region, imagination, courage and entrepreneurial spirit are tradition. Convince yourself of the advantages of the Dresden region. I am certain that we will also in future be pleased with the economic and technological successes in Dresden and Saxony.

Infrastruktur

Die Region Dresden baut aus
The Dresden region is developing

Dr. habil. Henry Hasenpflug
Der 1948 geborene Autor hat in Dresden Geografie und Mathematik auf Lehramt studiert. Nach der Promotion habilitierte er zu sozial- und wirtschaftsgeografischen Fragestellungen. Von 1992 bis 1998 zunächst im sächsischen Staatsministerium des Innern, war Hasenpflug bis 2000 Präsident des Statistischen Landesamtes des Freistaates. Er ist Präsident der Landesdirektion Dresden.
The author was born in 1948 and studied geography and mathematics in the German teacher education programme. After obtaining his doctorate he qualified as a professor in socio-economic geographical issues. From 1992 until 1998, he first worked at the Saxon State Ministry of Home Affairs and until 2000, he was the president of the Statistical State Office of Saxony. He is the president of the Dresden State Directorate.

**Auf neuen Wegen nach Osten –
Zur Entwicklung der Verkehrsinfrastruktur im Direktionsbezirk Dresden**
Der bedarfsgerechte Ausbau der Infrastruktur aller Verkehrsträger ist von zentraler Bedeutung für die wirtschaftliche Entwicklung einer Region. Als Planfeststellungsbehörde und als Bewilligungsstelle bei der Förderung von Verkehrsvorhaben ist die Landesdirektion Dresden an der Entwicklung der Verkehrsinfrastruktur im Direktionsbezirk Dresden mit beteiligt und übernimmt dabei eine Bündelungsfunktion.

Der Bund und der Freistaat Sachsen sehen sich insbesondere für die grundlegende verkehrliche Erschließung der Region in der Pflicht. Dabei erlangt die grenzüberschreitende Anbindung Ostsachsens nach Polen und Tschechien, gerade auch als Aspekt wachsender wirtschaftlicher Vernetzung und Abhängigkeit, zunehmendes Gewicht.

Die konzeptionelle Basis für den Aus- und Neubau der Bundesfernstraßen, der Schienenwege des Bundes und der Bundeswasserstraßen bilden der Bundesverkehrswegeplan 2001–2015 (BVWP), die Verkehrsprojekte Deutsche Einheit und der Landesentwicklungsplan des Freistaates Sachsen. Ein alle Verkehrsträger umfassender Investitionsrahmenplan legt ergänzend die mittelfristige Investitionsstrategie des Bundes zur Umsetzung der Verkehrspolitik für die Jahre 2006 bis 2010 fest und schafft für die Bundesländer die notwendige Planungs- und Investitionssicherheit.

Nach dem aktuell geltenden BVWP entfallen im Direktionsbezirk Dresden auf Bundesautobahnen und Bundesstraßen im vordringlichen Bedarf sowie im weiteren Bedarf dreißig Vorhaben mit veranschlagten Gesamtkosten von etwa 626 Millionen Euro. Bei diesen Maßnahmen handelt es sich im Wesentlichen um den Bau von Ortsumgehungen und den Ausbau von Autobahnanschlussstellen. Ziel der Maßnahmen ist die Beseitigung von Verkehrsengpässen und die Erschließung strukturschwacher Regionen. Gleichzeitig öffnet oder verbessert ein erheblicher Teil der Vorhaben Möglichkeiten des regionalen Grenzverkehrs zwischen Sachsen, Nordböhmen und Niederschlesien oder stellt Anschlüsse an große überregionale Verkehrsachsen her.

Schon in der Vergangenheit zielte eine Reihe von Vorhaben, die die Landesdirektion beziehungsweise das Regierungspräsidium Dresden als Planfeststellungs- und Förderstelle begleiteten, auf die verkehrliche Öffnung des Landes über seine östlichen Grenzen hinaus. Exemplarisch dafür ist der Neubau der Bundesautobahn A 17.

Infrastructure

Seit 2003 sind in Dresden die mit 45 Metern längsten Straßenbahnzüge der Welt – gebaut bei Bombardier in Bautzen – im Einsatz. Damit gelingt den Dresdner Verkehrsbetrieben ein wirtschaftlicher und kundenfreundlicher Kompromiss zwischen Taktzeit, Reisekomfort und Beförderungskapazität.
Since 2003, the longest commuter trains in the world with a length of 45 metres – built at Bombardier in Bautzen – are in use. Therewith the Dresden transportation companies succeed in an economic and client-friendly compromise between cycle time, travel comfort and carrying capacity.
Quelle/Source: Dresdner Verkehrsbetriebe AG

Breaking new ground to the East – The development of traffic infrastructure in the Dresden administrative county

The need-based extension of the infrastructure of all transport carriers is of central importance for the economic development of a region. The Dresden State Directorate, as the planning approval authority and the authorization body for the funding of traffic projects, is involved in the development of the traffic infrastructure in the Dresden administrative county and thereby assumes a bundling role.

The Federal Government and the Free State of Saxony regard themselves responsible particularly for the fundamental traffic development of the region. Thereby the East Saxon transnational connection to Poland and the Czech Republic gains increasing importance, especially also in terms of growing economic integration and dependency.

The conceptual basis for the development and new construction of the major federal motorways, the federal railroads and the federal waterways is formed by the Federal Route Plan 2001–2015 (BVWP-Bundesverkehrswegeplan), the Traffic Projects German Unity and the State Development Plan of the Free State of Saxony. An investment master plan which encompasses all transport carriers additionally stipulates the medium-term investment strategy of the Federation for the execution of transport policies for 2006 until 2010 and creates the necessary planning and investment security for the federal states.

According to the currently applicable Federal Route Plan, in the Dresden administrative county federal motorways and federal roads with an urgent demand as well as with other demand are accounted for by thirty projects with estimated total costs of approximately 626 million euros. These measures primarily concern the construction of bypasses and the development of motorway access points. The objective of these measures is the elimination of traffic congestion and the development of structurally underdeveloped regions. Simultaneously, a substantial part of the projects opens or improves the opportunities of regional border traffic between Saxony, North Bohemia and Lower Silesia or establishes junctions to large nationwide transport axes.

Already in the past, numerous projects which were accompanied by the State Directorate or the Dresden Regional Council as the official plan approving and funding body were aimed at the opening of state traffic over its eastern borders and beyond. An example thereof is the new construction of the A 17 federal motorway.

On the German side, the expressway to Prague has a length of 44.6 kilometres, for which the Dresden Regional Council executed the planning approval procedure. The traffic clearance was carried out on 21 December 2006. Therewith one of the most significant transport projects in the region was brought to a close: Starting with the preliminary draft plan in 1995 through the planning approval notice in 2003 up to the clearance, the project engaged the Dresden Regional Council for more than ten years.

Infrastruktur

Diesel- und Elektromotor kombiniert ein Hybridbus, den die Dresdner Verkehrsbetriebe seit 2008 im Stadtverkehr versuchsweise einsetzen, um die Eignung der Technologie für einen umweltschonenden und energieeffizienten ÖPNV unter Praxisbedingungen zu prüfen.
A diesel and electronic motor combined into a hybrid bus, which the Dresden transportation companies use in practice on a trial basis in order to test the suitability of the technology for an environmentally sound and energy-efficient local public transport.
Quelle/Source: Dresdner Verkehrsbetriebe AG

Auf deutschem Gebiet hat die Schnellstraße von Dresden nach Prag eine Länge von 44,6 Kilometern, für die das Dresdner Regierungspräsidium das Planfeststellungsverfahren durchgeführt hat. Die Verkehrsfreigabe erfolgte am 21. Dezember 2006. Damit war eines der bedeutendsten Verkehrsprojekte in der Region zum Abschluss gebracht worden: Angefangen von der Vorentwurfsplanung im Jahr 1995 über den Planfeststellungsbeschluss im Jahr 2003 bis zur Freigabe hat das Vorhaben das Regierungspräsidium Dresden mehr als zehn Jahre beschäftigt.

Auch der bereits dem Verkehr übergebene Abschnitt 1.2 der B 178n zwischen Nostitz und Löbau ist Teil einer wichtigen Verbindung zu den östlichen Nachbarn. Die Fernstraße wird nach ihrer Fertigstellung den gesamten südostsächsischen Raum zwischen Zittau und Löbau an die BAB 4 anbinden und gleichzeitig den Anschluss nach Liberec und weiter nach Prag herstellen.

Ein weiteres Beispiel der über die Regions- und Landesgrenzen hinaus wirksamen infrastrukturellen Aufwertung der Region ist der Neubau einer Start- und Landebahn für den Dresdner Flughafen. Im Zuge der Realisierung dieses Vorhabens im Jahr 2007 wurde die Piste bei laufendem Flugbetrieb verlegt und verlängert. Das erforderliche Planfeststellungsverfahren führte auch in diesem Falle das Dresdner Regierungspräsidium durch. Der Airport in Dresden entfaltet inzwischen auch Anziehungskraft für Fluggäste von jenseits der Landesgrenzen. 2008 wurden dort fast 37.000 Flugbewegungen registriert. Mit 1,86 Millionen Fluggästen erzielte der Dresdner Flughafen dabei im vergangenen Jahr erneut einen Rekord bei den Passagierzahlen.

Hinsichtlich ihrer Bilanz im Dienste der Verkehrsinfrastruktur der Region kann sich die Landesdirektion Dresden aber auch mit ihren Leistungen in jüngster Vergangenheit sehen lassen. In den Jahren zwischen 2006 und 2008 haben die Landesdirektion Dresden beziehungsweise die Vorgängerbehörde, das bis Juli 2008 bestehende Regierungspräsidium Dresden, in der Region unter anderem für folgende Vorhaben durch Planfeststellungsbeschlüsse Baurecht geschaffen:

- Bundesstraße 96/Bundesstraße 6 – Westtangente Bautzen: Diese Maßnahme zielt auf die Verlagerung des Durchgangsverkehr aus der Bautzener Innenstadt und führt zu einer Weiterentwicklung des Stadtrings.
- Neubau Staatsstraße 106, Südumgehung Bautzen: Damit gelingt die Verknüpfung der auf Bautzen zulaufenden Staats- und Bundesstraßen durch einen Straßenring und ein schnellerer Autobahnzugang.
- Bundesstraße 98, Ortsumfahrung Bischofswerda: Das Vorhaben verspricht eine leistungsfähige Verbindung zwischen Kamenz, Sebnitz, Neustadt und Bischofswerda, garantiert zudem eine schnellere Anbindung der Sächsischen Schweiz an BAB 4.
- Neubau der Bundesstraße 178n, Abschnitt 3.1 zwischen Löbau und Obercunnersdorf: Der abschnittsweise erfolgende Neubau dieser in Nord-Süd-Richtung verlaufenden Fernstraße ist von überragender Bedeutung für den ostsächsischen Raum; die Trasse bindet das Dreiländereck an das deutsche Autobahnnetz an und erschließt dabei insbesondere auch den nordböhmischen Raum.
- Neubau der Staatsstraße S 127b, Zubringer und Grenzübergang Krauschwitz: Damit gelingt die Entlastung des in Bad Muskau gelegenen Grenzübergangs, mithin die Verbesserung der regionalen Verkehrsanbindungen von der und in die Republik Polen.
- Ausbau der Bundesstraße B 170 südlich Dippoldiswalde: Leistungsfähigkeit und Verkehrssicherheit der Bundesstraße, die als Europastraße E 55 eine der wichtigen Verbindungen der Grenzregion südlich von Dresden mit dem Autobahnnetz anbietet, werden deutlich verbessert; gleichzeitig erfolgt die Anpassung an den erforderlichen Hochwasserschutz.

Infrastructure

Verkehrsträger verknüpfen, Anschlüsse vertakten, Fahrgäste informieren – Übergangstellen wie hier in Hirschfelde bei Görlitz sind Voraussetzung für einen attraktiven ÖPNV.
Connecting transport, synchronizing junctions, informing passengers – Transition points such as these in Hirschfelde near Görlitz are prerequisites for an attractive local public transport.

Quelle/Source: ZVON

The section 1.2 of the B178n between Nostitz and Löbau, which has already been released to traffic, is a part of the important connection to eastern neighbours. After its completion, the high way will connect the entire south-eastern Saxony region between Zittau and Löbau to federal motorway 4 and simultaneously establish the connection to Liberec and further on to Prague.

Another example of the effective infrastructural upgrading of the region over the regional and state borders and beyond is the new construction of a runway for the Dresden International Airport. In the course of the implementation of this project in 2007, the runway was relocated and extended during ongoing air traffic. The necessary planning approval procedure was also in this case executed by the Dresden Regional Council. In the meantime, the airport in Dresden has also developed an attraction for air passengers from beyond the state borders. In 2008, almost 37,000 flight operations were registered there. Last year, with 1.86 million passengers, the Dresden International Airport therewith again achieved a record in passenger volume.

As regards its record in the service of the traffic infrastructure of the region, the Dresden State Directorate can be proud, however, also with its performance in the recent past. In the years between 2006 and 2008, the Dresden State Directorate, or rather its predecessor authority, the Dresden Regional Council, which existed until July 2008, created building rights through planning approval notices for the following projects, amongst others in the region:

- Federal road 96/federal road 6 – Westtangente Bautzen: This scheme aims at the shifting of transit traffic out of the Bautzen city centre and leads to an enhancement of the city ring road.
- New construction of state road 106, Bautzen southern bypass: Therewith, the connection of the state and federal roads which run towards Bautzen via a road ring and an express motorway access, is successful.
- Federal road 98, Bischofswerda eastern bypass: The project assures an effective connection between Kamenz, Sebnitz, Neustadt and Bischofswerda, and in addition guarantees an express connection of Saxon Switzerland to federal motorway 4.
- New construction of federal road 178n, section 3.1 between Löbau and Obercunnersdorf: The progressive new construction of this major motorway, which runs in a north-south direction, is of paramount significance to the East Saxon region; the route links the border triangle to the German motorway network and therewith in particular, also opens up the North Bohemian region.
- New construction of state road S 127b, feeder and the border crossing at Krauschwitz: Therewith, the relief of the border crossing situated in Bad Muskau and consequently the improvement of the regional traffic connections from and to Poland, is successful.
- New construction of federal road B 170 south of Dippoldiswalde: The capacity and road safety of the federal road, which as the Europastraße (International E-road network) E 55 offers one of the most important connections of the border region south of Dresden to the motorway network, are markedly being improved; simultaneously, the adaptation to the required flood protection is being carried out.

Infrastruktur

Quelle/Source: Flughafen Dresden GmbH/Michael Weimer

- Ausbau der B 156 zwischen Bautzen und der ehemaligen Kreisgrenze Kamenz zur Stärkung der Verkehrsverbindung Bautzen – Hoyerswerda und weiter nach Bad Muskau.
- Ausbau der B 115 Görlitz – Cottbus in und südlich von Weißkeißel: Verkehrsströme, die aus dem Süden durch die B 178 zunächst bis zur BAB 4 bei Weißenberg geführt werden, kann die leistungsfähigere Trasse aufnehmen und als Querspange zu BAB 15 weiterleiten.

Gegenwärtig werden für insgesamt 68 weitere Vorhaben Anträge auf Planfeststellung in der Landesdirektion Dresden bearbeitet. Unter diesen Vorhaben sind wieder einige, die auch auf eine bessere infrastrukturelle Vernetzung mit den osteuropäischen Nachbarn zielen.

So läuft für die bereits mehrfach erwähnte B 178n nun die Planfeststellung für die Abschnitte 3.2 und 3.3, mit denen unter Umgehung des Nadelöhrs Herrnhut die Neubautrasse bis nahe an Zittau heran verlängert werden soll.

Auch für eine neue Erdgasfernleitung, die Sachsen von Nord nach Süd queren soll, ist die Landesdirektion Dresden als Planfeststeller gegenwärtig tätig. Dieser OPAL (Ostsee-Pipeline-Anbindungs-Leitung) genannte Energiestrang soll künftig dafür sorgen, dass Erdgas aus Russland, unter Umgehung störanfälliger Landtransite, durch die Ostsee direkt bis nach Deutschland und von dort weiter nach Süd- und Westeuropa strömen kann. Das Vorhaben hat mithin für die Sicherheit der Energieversorgung der gesamten Europäischen Union Bedeutung.

Aber nicht nur im grenznahen östlichen, sondern auch im westlichen Teil des Direktionsbezirkes beteiligt sich die Landesdirektion Dresden mit laufenden Planfeststellungsverfahren an den Vorbereitungen für weitere wichtige Verbesserungen der Infrastruktur. Beispielsweise kann mit der abschnittsweisen Planfeststellung für den Neubau der B 169 zwischen Riesa und der BAB 14 für eine leistungsfähige Anbindung der gesamten Wirtschaftsregion Riesa an das europäische Fernstraßennetz gesorgt werden.

Mobilität wirtschaftlich und ökologisch organisieren – Zum Ausbau des öffentlichen Personennahverkehrs im Direktionsbezirk Dresden

Der öffentliche Personennahverkehr (ÖPNV) trägt sowohl zur Bewältigung der großen Verkehrsströme in den Ballungsgebieten als auch zur mobilen Grundversorgung in den schwächer besiedelten Gebieten des Direktionsbezirkes Dresden bei. Die Landesdirektion Dresden unterstützt die Bemühungen der Verkehrsunternehmen, Zweckverbände und Kommunen um einen attraktiven und bezahlbaren ÖPNV unter anderen durch die Gewährung von Fördermitteln. Allein in den Jahren 2007 und 2008 wurden hierfür Zuwendungen von insgesamt etwa 167 Millionen Euro ausgereicht.

Einen Schwerpunkt bildete dabei die Fortsetzung des Ausbaus der S-Bahn-Linie zwischen Pirna und Meißen im Bereich des Bahnhofs Dresden-Neustadt.

In der Umsetzung ist die Modernisierung der Eisenbahnstrecke zwischen Bischofswerda und Zittau. Mit Investitionen von etwa 85 Millionen Euro wird hier die Voraussetzung in den Bereichen Oberbau, Ingenieurbau und Sicherungstechnik geschaffen, um die Entfernung von Dresden-Neustadt nach Zittau in weniger als 80 Minuten zurückzulegen und gleichzeitig eine schnelle Verbindung zu unseren tschechischen Nachbarn herzustellen.

2007 wurde auch mit den Arbeiten an der Eisenbahnstrecke zwischen Görlitz und Zittau begonnen, um eine den heutigen Anforderungen genügende Beförderungsqualität anbieten zu können. Dies beinhaltet auch den Bau neuer Zugangsstellen in Hirschfelde und Hagenwerder.

Infrastructure

Airport Dresden 2008: Die alte Landebahn wird abgebrochen, während die neue – schmaler, aber länger – schon in Betrieb ist. Der Flughafen bietet den Airlines jetzt größere Reichweiten, weil Mittelstreckenmaschinen nun auch voll betankt rechtzeitig vom Boden kommen.
Dresden International Airport 2008: The old runway is being demolished, while the new one – narrower, but longer – is already in operation. The airport now offers the airlines larger operating distances, because medium-range aircrafts can now also take off fully refuelled.

- Development of the B 156 between Bautzen and the old Kamenz county boundary for the strengthening of the Bautzen – Hoyersverda traffic connection and further to Bad Muskau.
- New construction of the Görlitz – Cottbus B 115 in and to the south of Weißkeißel: Traffic flows, which are initially routed from the south via the B 178 up to federal motorway 4 at Weißenberg, can take up the more efficient roadway and transfer as a link road to federal road 15.

At present, a total of 68 further project applications are being processed for planning approval at the Dresden State Directorate. Amongst these projects are again some which are also aimed at a better infrastructural cross-linking with the East European neighbours.

Thus, the planning approval for sections 3.2 and 3.3 for the repeatedly mentioned B 178n is now already underway, with which the newly constructed road is to be extended close up to Zittau, avoiding the Herrnhut bottleneck.
The Dresden State Directorate as the planning approver is also currently busy with a new natural gas pipeline, which is to cross Saxony from north to south. This so-called OPAL (Ostsee-Pipeline-Anbindungs-Leitung – Baltic Sea Pipeline Connection Pipe) energy line is to ensure the future flow of natural gas from Russia through the Baltic Sea directly to Germany and from there further on to South and West Europe, avoiding accident-sensitive land transit. The project therefore has significance for the security of energy supply of the entire European Union.

However, the Dresden State Directorate is involved not only in the east, which is close to the border, but also in the western part of the administrative county, in on-going planning approval procedures in preparation for further important improvements of the infrastructure. For instance, the progressive planning approval for the new construction of the B 169 between Riesa and federal motorway 14 provides for an effective connection of the entire Riesa economic region to the European high way network.

Mobility economically and ecologically organized – The development of local public transport in the Dresden administrative county

The local public transport (ÖPNV) contributes towards the coverage of large traffic flows in the urban centres as well as to mobile basic services in the poorly populated areas of the Dresden administrative county. The Dresden State Directorate supports the efforts of transport organizations, administrative unions and town councils for an attractive and affordable local public transportation amongst other things through the granting of funding. In 2007 and 2008 alone, grants totalling 167 million euros were extended for this purpose.
In the process, a focal point is provided for the continuation of the development of the commuter train line between Pirna and Meißen in the area of the Dresden-Neustadt railway station.

The modernization of the railway line between Bischofswerda and Zittau is in the process of implementation. With investments of around 85 million euros, the preconditions in the super-structural, civil engineering and security technology areas are created, in order to cover the distance between Dresden-Neustadt and Zittau in less than 80 minutes and simultaneously provide a speedy connection to our Czech neighbours.

In 2007, work also began on the railway line between Görlitz and Zittau to be able to offer transportation qualities sufficing present day requirements. This also comprises the construction of new entry points in Hirschfelde and Hagenwerder.

Infrastruktur

Mit einer aufwendigen Tunnel-Brücke-Tunnel-Kombination führt die Autobahn nach Prag über das im Dresdner Süden gelegene Flusstal der Weißeritz.
With a complex tunnel-bridge-tunnel combination, the motorway leads to Prague via the Weißeritz river valley, which is situated in the south of Dresden.

Die Landeshauptstadt Dresden bildet nach wie vor einen bedeutenden Schwerpunkt des Investitionsgeschehens im Verkehrssektor. Mit dem Ausbau des Lennéplatzes wurde eine weitere große Maßnahme der Dresdner Verkehrsbetriebe AG im Bereich Verkehrsanlagen realisiert. Im übrigen Streckennetz konzentrierten sich die Arbeiten in den letzten Jahren vor allem auf den Abschluss der Beseitigung der Flutschäden des Jahres 2002 sowie die barrierefreie Gestaltung von Haltestellenanlagen.

Höhepunkt des Baugeschehens für die Dresdner Straßenbahn war jedoch die Inbetriebnahme der gemeinsam mit dem Bau der Anschlussstelle der Bundesstraße 173 an die BAB 17 realisierten Verlängerung der Straßenbahntrasse der Linie 7 von Dresden-Gorbitz nach Dresden-Gompitz mit einer Länge von circa 2,7 Kilometern.

Im Bereich der Busverkehrsunternehmen ist die Modernisierung der Betriebsanlagen abgeschlossen. Hier konzentrieren sich die Anstrengungen nunmehr auf die Einführung neuer Kommunikations- und Abfertigungstechnik. Im Jahr 2008 beginnend, wird es künftig in Umsetzung der Ergebnisse des Forschungsvorhabens „intermobil Region Dresden" ein regionales Betriebsleitsystem geben, das sowohl die Verknüpfung der einzelnen Verkehrsmittel sichert als auch der verkehrsträgerübergreifenden Information der Fahrgäste dient.

Dieses System wird umso wirksamer, je mehr und bessere Verknüpfungsstellen zwischen den einzelnen Anbietern des ÖPNV einerseits und dem Individualverkehr andererseits geschaffen werden. Die Investitionsprogramme der Zweckverbände Verkehrsverbund Oberelbe (ZVOE) und Oberlausitz-Niederschlesien (ZVON), die etwa 60 Vorhaben für Umsteigestellen im Direktionsbezirk beinhalten, sollen bis 2010 im Wesentlichen abgeschlossen sein. In den letzten zwei Jahren kamen die Übergangsstellen beziehungsweise Busbahnhöfe und P+R-Anlagen in Glashütte, Dresden-Cossebaude, Bischofswerda, Dürrröhrsdorf, Priestewitz, Großhartau, Pulsnitz, Radeberg, Ottendorf-Okrilla und Pirna hinzu. Im Bau befinden sich Anlagen in Arnsdorf, Klingenberg-Colmnitz und Riesa. Sie werden gemeinsam mit den in den nächsten Jahren noch fertig zu stellenden Verknüpfungsstellen dazu beitragen, dass die Zahl der ÖPNV-Nutzer, die trotz des Bevölkerungsrückganges zum Beispiel im Jahr 2007 gegenüber dem Vorjahr um circa zwei Prozent zunahm, weiter steigt.

Ein moderner ÖPNV wird natürlich auch durch den Einsatz moderner Fahrzeuge geprägt. So wurde die Förderung der Beschaffung von Omnibussen mit jährlich circa sechs Millionen Euro fortgeführt. Die Dresdner Verkehrsbetriebe AG wird ab 2010 in der Lage sein, ausschließlich moderne Niederflur-Straßenbahnen aus Bautzen einzusetzen. Bereits seit 2007 verkehren im S-Bahn-Bereich Dresden 53 neue Doppelstockwagen, die in der ebenfalls neu entstandenen Fahrzeugwerkstatt Dresden-Altstadt gepflegt und instandgehalten werden können.

Ein weiteres Anliegen unseres Hauses ist die Förderung attraktiverer und sicherer Haltestellen des ÖPNV in der Region, stellen diese doch das unmittelbare Bindeglied zwischen Fahrgast und Verkehrsunternehmen dar. In den Kommunen wurden mit dem Bau von jährlich 20 bis 30 Haltestellen und Fahrgastunterständen bereits spürbare Verbesserungen erreicht. Gemeinsam mit den Zweckverbänden werden wir diesen Weg weiter beschreiten.

Infrastructure

Öffentlicher Nahverkehr braucht einen attraktiven Fahrzeugpark: Durch das Elbtal zwischen Dresden und dem nahe gelegenen Nationalpark Sächsische Schweiz verkehren seit 2007 klimatisierte S-Bahn-Züge.
Local public transport requires an attractive vehicle pool: Since 2007, air-conditioned commuter trains run through the Elbe Valley between Dresden and the nearby Saxon Switzerland National Park.

The state capital of Dresden still forms a significant focal point of investment activities in the transportation sector. With the development of the Lennéplatz, a further great scheme of the Dresdner Verkehrsbetriebe AG (a public transportation company) in the traffic facility area was implemented. In the remaining route network the work, in the last few years has, above all, been concentrated on the completion of the removal of the flood damage of 2002, as well on as the obstacle-free design of bus stop facilities.

However, the highlight of the construction activities for the Dresden tram line was the start of the extension of the tramline section of line 7 from Dresden-Gorbitz to Dresden-Gompitz with a length of approximately 2.7 kilometres, that was jointly realized with the construction of the connection point of federal road 173 to federal motorway 17.

In the range of the bus transportation companies, the modernization of the operational facilities has been concluded. Here, efforts are henceforth concentrated on the introduction of new communication and dispatch technology. Commencing in 2008, at the realization of the findings of the research project "intermobil", in future there is to be a regional operations control system in the Dresden region, which will ensure the connection of individual means of transport as well as serving the overlapping transport carrier information of passengers.

This system will become all the more effective, the more and the better the connection points which are created between the individual providers of the ÖPNV on the one hand, and the individual traffic on the other hand. The investment programmes of the Zweckverbände Verkehrsverbund Oberelbe (ZVOE – Transport Federation Upper Elbe) and Oberlausitz-Niederschlesien (ZVON – Transport Federation Upper Lusatia-Lower Silesia), which contain about 60 projects for transfer points in the administrative county, should in essence be completed by 2010. In the past two years, the transition point or rather, bus stations and PR facilities, were added in Glashütte, Dresden-Cossebaude, Bischofswerda, Dürrröhrsdorf, Priestewitz, Großhartau, Pulsnitz, Radeberg, Ottendorf-Okrilla and Pirna. Facilities under construction are found in Arnsdorf, Klingenberg-Colmnitz and Riesa. Together with the connection points which are to be completed in the next few years, they will contribute thereto that the number of ÖPNV (local public transport) users will increase further, which despite the decline in population, for instance from the previous year, increased by about two per cent in 2007.

A modern ÖPNV is naturally also characterized by the application of modern vehicles. In this way, the promotion of the acquisition of omnibuses is continued with approximately six million euros per annum. From 2010 onward the Dresdner Verkehrsbetriebe AG will be in a position to utilize only modern low-floor trams from Bautzen. In Dresden, already since 2007, in the commuter train area, 53 new double-deck coaches have been in operation, which can be cleaned and maintained in the likewise newly created Fahrzeugwerkstatt Dresden-Altstadt (vehicle workshop).

A further concern of our office is the promotion of attractive and safe ÖPNV stations in the region, as these represent the direct link between the passenger and the transport company. In the local councils visible improvements have already been achieved with the annual construction of 20 to 30 stations and passenger shelters. In conjunction with the administrative union we will continue making further progress in this regard.

Drehscheibe und wichtigste Verkehrsinfrastruktur für die Region
A hub and an important transportation infrastructure for the region

Dr. Michael Hupe
Der 1964 in Seattle (USA) geborene Wirtschaftsingenieur ist Geschäftsführer der Flughafen Dresden GmbH. Studiert und promoviert hat Dr. Hupe an der Technischen Universität Darmstadt. Von 1995 bis 1998 arbeitete er als Projektmanager bei der Kreditanstalt für Wiederaufbau im Bereich Flugzeug- und Flughafenfinanzierung. Später leitete er bis 2002 bei der Fraport AG die Konzernfinanzierung.

The author, born in Seattle (USA) in 1964, is an industrial engineer and the Gerneral Manager of the Dresden International Airport. Dr. Hupe studied and obtained his doctorate at the Technische Universität Darmstadt. From 1995 to 1998, he worked as a project manager at the Kreditanstalt für Wiederaufbau in the area of aircraft and airport financing. Later, he was head of corporate financing at the Fraport AG.

Forschung und Entwicklung funktionieren heutzutage im Wesentlichen in Netzwerken. Kooperation und Kommunikation sind Grundvoraussetzung für den Erfolg. Entgegen der These aus dem letzten Jahrzehnt, dass die Entwicklung der modernen Telekommunikation mit Bildtelefonie und „virtuellen Meetings" das Reisen überflüssig machen würde, ist der umgekehrte Effekt eingetreten: Die Menschen suchen den persönlichen Kontakt, Forschungsgruppen etablieren sich auf Zeit an einem Ort, Konferenzen bleiben eine wichtige Säule des fachlichen Gedankenaustausches.

Insofern ist bei einer internationalen, vielfach globalen Arbeitsteilung Mobilität ein wichtiger Produktions-, ja Produktivitätsfaktor. Diese Mobilität kann bei Entfernungen über circa 400 Kilometer effizient nur durch Luftverkehr dargestellt werden.

Anders als im touristisch geprägten Charterverkehr, bei dem der Reisende in Bezug auf Zielgebiet und Zeitpunkt disponieren kann, ist der Passagier im Geschäftsreiseverkehr nicht flexibel. Termin und Ort sind fest vorgegeben und sollen mit geringem zeitlichem Vor- und Nachlauf abgebildet sowie mit kurzer Reisezeit erreicht werden. Dies stellt andere Anforderungen an die Qualität von Flugverbindungen als der Tourismus. Benötigt werden hohe Frequenzen und eine große Auswahl an Endzielen.

Ein attraktives Netz an Interkontinentalverbindungen wird in Europa von weniger als zehn Flughäfen, den sogenannten Hubs, angeboten. Neben dem Aufkommen der Region selbst – alle Hubs liegen im Einzugsgebiet großer Städte oder wirtschaftlich starker Regionen – wird ein zusätzliches Aufkommen in Form von Umsteigeverkehr von Sekundärflughäfen generiert. Nur dieser rechtfertigt den Einsatz von großen Langstreckenflugzeugen.

Für die Sekundärflughäfen ist es daher wichtig, effizient über Hubs an das internationale Luftverkehrsnetz angebunden zu sein. Kriterium sind dabei die Anzahl der Verbindungen pro Tag, um kurze Umsteigezeiten realisieren zu können. Als Minimum gelten dabei drei tägliche Verbindungen.

Der Flughafen Dresden kann eine Vielzahl solcher Verbindungen darstellen. Die beiden wichtigsten Hubs Deutschlands, Frankfurt und München, werden bis zu siebenmal täglich angeflogen. Auch Wien und Zürich werden dreimal täglich bedient. Damit lassen sich viele Anschlussflüge mit Umsteigezeiten von 60 bis 90 Minuten innereuropäisch und interkontinental erreichen.

Airport

Trockenen Fußes vom Terminal ins Parkhaus – der Skywalk am Flughafen Dresden.
Dry feet from the terminal into the car park – the skywalk at the Dresden Airport.

Today, research and development are organized primarily in networks. Cooperation and communication are basic requirements for success. Contrary to the assumption of the previous decade, that the development of modern telecommunication with video telephony and virtual meetings" would make travelling redundant, the opposite effect has occurred. People are looking for personal contact, research groups establish themselves in one place temporarily and conferences remain an important pillar for the professional exchange of ideas.

In this respect, mobility is an important production factor, even more a productivity factor, in an internationally diverse, often global division of labour. At distances of more than 400 kilometres, this mobility can only be efficiently assured by air travel.

Unlike the charter traffic serving tourists, in which travellers are able to choose destination and time, the business traveller is less flexible. Date and place are fixed and should be met with minor pre- and post-flight time lags as well as being achievable within short travelling times. This leads to other requirements on the quality of flight connections than in tourism. High frequencies and a large selection of final destinations are required.

An attractive range of intercontinental destinations is offered in Europe by less than ten airports – the so-called hubs. Besides the amount of passengers of the region itself, all hubs are located in the catchment area of large cities or economically strong regions, an additional amount of passengers in form of transfer traffic is generated from secondary airports. This alone justifies the operation of long-haul aircrafts.

For the secondary airports it is therefore important to be connected to the international air traffic network efficiently via hubs. Criteria for this are the number of flights per day in order to realise short connecting times. Three flights per day are regarded as the minimum.

Dresden Airport is able to offer a vast number of such connections. The two most important hubs of Germany, Frankfurt and Munich, can be reached up to seven times a day. Vienna and Zurich are also served three times daily. Thereby many connecting flights with transfer times of 60 to 90 minutes are reachable within Europe or inter-continentally.

The airport therewith fulfils its task as the most important transportation infrastructure for the research and economic location of Dresden.

Auf der Eventebene lassen sich Kongresse mit bis zu 700 Teilnehmern und Musikveranstaltungen mit bis zu 1.400 Teilnehmern durchführen.
On the events level, congresses housing up to 700 participants and musical events with up to 1,400 participants are accomplished.

Das Transportflugzeug Beluga lieferte am 10.10.2008 den Rumpf eines Airbus A320 an die EADS Elbe Flugzeugwerke aus.
On 10.10.2008, the Beluga air freighter delivered the fuselage of an Airbus A320 to the EADS Elbe Flugzeugwerke (aircraft works).

Der Flughafen erfüllt damit seine Aufgabe als wichtigste Verkehrsinfrastruktur für den Forschungs- und Wirtschaftsstandort Dresden.

An weiteren (europäischen) Direktverbindungen wird intensiv gearbeitet. Der Nachweis eines ausreichenden Verkehrsaufkommens zu deren Rechtfertigung ist aber aufgrund der geringen Größe des Einzugsgebiets und der geringen Kaufkraft, insbesondere aber mangels bedeutender Firmenzentralen und reiseintensiver Dienstleistungen, nur für einige wenige Ziele möglich.

Erkenntnisse über den Bedarf von wissenschaftlichen Instituten und Industrie erhält der Flughafen durch Analysen der Endziele abfliegender Passagiere, Unternehmensbefragungen in Zusammenarbeit mit Wirtschaftsförderung und IHK sowie Auswertungen von Daten der Reisebüros. Die Entwicklung des interkontinentalen Aufkommens in den letzten fünf Jahren ist beachtlich. So betrug das Wachstum nach Asien kumuliert 74 Prozent und nach Nordamerika 25 Prozent.

Um den Luftverkehr effizient, sicher und für den Reisenden bequem abwickeln zu können, wurde am Flughafen in den letzten zehn Jahren viel getan. 2001 wurde ein neues Terminal zusammen mit einem Parkhaus mit 1.500 Stellplätzen in Betrieb genommen. Mit einem eigenen Autobahnanschluss und einem S-Bahnhof direkt im Terminal ist der Flughafen optimal intermodal angebunden. Dies garantiert kurze Wege und eine schnelle An- und Abreise. Der Flughafen sichert so ab, dass der Passagier die Zeit, die er in der Luft gewinnt, nicht am Boden wieder verliert. Regelmäßig durchgeführte Umfragen zeigen, dass der Fluggast dies sehr zu schätzen weiß.

Die 2007 grunderneuerte und verlängerte Start- und Landebahn wird dauerhaft ein stabiles Rückgrat für die Abwicklung des Luftverkehrs bilden.

Airport

Das Großraumflugzeug Airbus A380 bei einem Testanflug (touch and go) auf dem Flughafen Dresden.
The wide-bodied Airbus A380 during a test landing (touch and go) at the Dresden Airport.

Für den Allwetterflugbetrieb nach Kategorie IIIb ausgerüstet, können Flugzeuge auch bei schlechtem Wetter sicher landen.
For the all-weather air traffic, according to category IIIb, it is possible to land aircrafts safely even in bad weather conditions.

Additional (European) direct connections are intensively being worked on. Evidence of sufficient demand for their justification is only possible for a couple of destinations, due to the limited size of the catchment area and the below average purchasing power, in combination with the lack of prominent company headquarters and travel-intensive services.

The airport obtains knowledge regarding the demand of scientific institutions and industry through the analysis of final destinations of departing passengers, company surveys in collaboration with economic development corporations and chambers of commerce as well as the evaluation of data from travel agencies. The development of intercontinental passengers in the past five years has been considerable. During that period the accumulated growth to Asia accounts for 74 per cent and to North America 25 per cent.

In order to manage air transport efficiently, safely and comfortably for travellers, much has been done at the airport in the past ten years. In 2001, a new terminal along with a car park housing 1,500 parking spaces was put into operation. With its own motorway exit and a commuter railway station within the terminal building, the airport has an optimal intermodal connection. This guarantees short distances and a speedy arrival and departure. The airport thus ensures that the time the passenger gains in the air, is not lost on the ground. Regularly conducted surveys show that this is highly appreciated by passengers.

The runway, which was rebuilt and extended in 2007, will form a stable backbone for the handling of air traffic for many years. Including planning, application and project approval this ambitious project was implemented in merely three years. With a length of 2,850 metres, the runway is sufficiently sized for the route network of the airport, which is characterized by short and medium-haul traffic. Intercontinental flights are also possible, however with restrictions regarding payload and range for some types of aircraft.

Significant innovations are taking place below the surface. In cooperation with the airlines, the technical basis for internet and automated check-in has been implemented. This makes the lead time before the flight shorter and more flexible. With a separate area for general aviation, the airport is also well-equipped for business charter traffic.

Inklusive Planung und Genehmigung wurde dieses ambitionierte Projekt in lediglich drei Jahren realisiert. Mit 2.850 Metern Länge ist die Bahn für das durch Kurz- und Mittelstreckenverkehr geprägte Streckennetz des Flughafens ausreichend dimensioniert. Auch Interkontinentalflüge sind möglich, allerdings bei einigen Flugzeugtypen mit Beschränkungen bei Nutzlast oder Reichweite.

Wesentliche Neuerungen finden hinter den Kulissen statt. In Kooperation mit den Airlines wurde die Möglichkeit des Internet- und Automaten-Check-ins etabliert. Dies verkürzt und flexibilisiert den zeitlichen Vorlauf vor dem Flug. Auch für den Business-Charter-Verkehr ist der Flughafen mit einem separaten Bereich für die Allgemein-Luftfahrt gut gerüstet.

Aufgrund der Kubatur des Terminals, das durch die Umgestaltung einer historischen Fertigungshalle der DDR-Luftfahrtindustrie entstand, konnten in das Gebäude Konferenzräume und eine große Veranstaltungsebene integriert werden. Damit wurde ein Angebot für Seminare und mittelgroße Kongresse für bis zu 700 Teilnehmer geschaffen, das nicht nur von Unternehmen der Nachbarschaft, sondern aus dem gesamten Dresdner Raum genutzt wird.

Auch dieses Produkt profitiert von der guten infrastrukturellen Erschließung des Flughafens mit schnellen Anfahrtswegen und ausreichend Parkraum.

Die umliegende Industrie ist ebenfalls Nutznießer der Entwicklung der Infrastruktur. Im Dresdner Norden, dem direkten Umfeld des Flughafens, haben sich in mehreren Industriegebieten viele Hightech-Unternehmen angesiedelt. Auch die Luftfahrtindustrie kann an alte Glanzzeiten anknüpfen. Der Umbau von älteren Passagier- zu Frachtflugzeugen, Dauerstabilitätstests von Flugzeugstrukturen und die Fertigung von Komponenten erfolgen direkt am Flughafen. Inklusive der Luftfahrtindustrie sind derzeit 2.900 Mitarbeiter am Standort tätig.

Airport 25

Während des Bauprojekts für die neue Start- und Landebahn existierten kurzfristig zwei Bahnen nebeneinander.
During the construction project for the new take-off and landing runway, two parallel airstrips were temporarily available.

Mit dem Terminalneubau 2001 wurde eine moderne, leistungsfähige Infrastruktur geschaffen.
With the building of the new terminal in 2001, a modern, efficient infrastructure was created.

As a result of the size of the terminal, which arose from the reconstruction of a historical production hangar of the GDR aircraft industry, conference rooms and a large event level could be integrated into the building. Therewith, a range of seminars and medium-sized conferences for up to 700 participants can be served, which is not only used by companies of the neighbourhood, but of the entire Dresden area. This product benefits also from the infrastructure of the airport, having fast access routes and sufficient parking space.

The surrounding industry is likewise a beneficiary of the development of the infrastructure. In the north of Dresden, the direct environment of the airport, many high-tech companies have settled in several industrial areas. The aviation industry can also relate to the good old days. The modification of older passenger aircrafts to air freighters, fatigue tests of aircraft structures and the manufacture of components take place right next to the airport. With the inclusion of the aviation industry, 2,900 people are currently employed at the site.

Company Profile

**Nehlsen-BWB
Flugzeug-Galvanik Dresden
GmbH & Co. KG**

Geschäftsführer/Managers:
Birgit Fischer
Stefan Kaßner

Gründungsjahr/Year of foundation:
1998/2004

Mitarbeiter/Employees:
125 Beschäftigte inkl. Auszubildende
125 employees including trainees

Geschäftstätigkeit/Business activity:
Betrieb einer Galvanik,
insbesondere für Flugzeugteile
• Verkupfern, Vernickeln, Verchromen,
Vercadmen, Verzinken,
Verzinnen, Versilbern
• Chemisch Vernickeln, Phosphatieren,
Brünieren, Gelbchromatieren (Al),
Chromitieren (RoHS-konform)
• Anod. Oxidieren (Eloxal), Hartanodisieren,
Chromsäureanodisieren
• Lackieren
Operating an electroplating shop,
especially for aircraft components
• copper-plating, nickel-plating, chromium-plating, cadmium-plating, galvanizing,
tin-plating, silver-plating
• electroless nickel plating, phosphating,
browning, yellow chromate coatings,
chromating (RoHS Certificate of Conformity)
• anod. oxidizing (eloxal), hard anodizing,
chromic acid anodizing
• varnishing

Jahresumsatz/Annual turnover:
12 Millionen Euro
12 million euros

Anschrift/Address:
Grenzstraße 2
D-01109 Dresden
Telefon +49 (0) 351 8831-400
Telefax +49 (0) 351 8831-404
info@flugzeuggalvanik.de
www.flugzeuggalvanik.de

**Bundesweit führend auf dem Gebiet der
Galvanik für die Luftfahrttechnologie.
The nationwide leader in the area
of electroplating for aviation technology.**

Kompetenz nicht nur im Bereich der Luft- und Raumfahrt
Competency not only in the ambit of aerospace

Die am Flughafen Dresden-Klotzsche ansässige Nehlsen-BWB Flugzeug-Galvanik Dresden GmbH & Co. KG ist ein High-tech-Unternehmen der Oberflächenschutz-Branche, das seit fast 50 Jahren am Standort existiert. Der frühere Betriebsteil der ehemaligen Flugzeugwerft Dresden gehört heute zur Schweizer BWB-Gruppe. In den vergangenen zehn Jahren ist es dem Unternehmen gelungen, sich zum führenden Zulieferer für Oberflächenschutz im Luftfahrtbereich mit der bundesweit größten luftfahrtzertifizierten Verfahrenspalette (DIN ISO 9001:2000 (QMS); EN 9100; EAA/EURAS-Gütesiegel QUALANOD) zu entwickeln. Über die Luftfahrttechnik hinaus wissen auch viele Betriebe des Maschinenbaus, der Fahrzeug- und Elektroindustrie sowie der Halbleiterindustrie das umfassende Leistungsangebot zu schätzen. Die Nehlsen-BWB Flugzeug-Galvanik ist damit einer der führenden Anbieter hochwertiger funktioneller Beschichtungen für die verschiedensten technischen Anwendungszwecke. Jüngste Highlights sind die Erweiterung der Kapazitäten bei chemischem Nickel und die spezielle Hartanodisieranlage, mit der bis zu 3,5 Tonnen schwere Aluminium-Werkzeuge und Laminierformen keramisch hart und verschleißfest beschichtet werden können. Auch für die kommenden Jahre setzt man hier auf ein kontinuierliches Wachstum und kooperative Forschung.

The Nehlsen-BWB Flugzeug-Galvanik Dresden GmbH & Co. KG, located at the Dresden-Klotzsche Airport, is a high-tech company in the surface-protection industry, which has been in existence at the location for almost 50 years. Today the previous plant section of the former aircraft works in Dresden belongs to the Swiss BWB Holding. For the past ten years, the company has been successfully developing itself into a leading supplier of surface-protection in the field of aviation with the largest range of aviation-accredited processes nationwide (DIN ISO 9001:2000 (QMS); EN 9100; EAA/EURAS Seal of approval QUALANOD). Also beyond aviation technology, many enterprises in the mechanical engineering, automotive and electronic industry as well as the semiconductor industry have come to value the comprehensive service offering. Nehlsen-BWB Flugzeug-Galvanik is therewith the leading provider of premium functional coatings for numerous application purposes. The latest highlights are the expansion of capacities in electroless nickel plating and the special hard anodizing facility, which can be used for ceramic bond and wear-resistant coating of aluminium implements and laminating moulds weighing up to 3.5 tonnes. Also for the coming years, the focus is placed on continual growth and co-operative research.

Company Profile

Spezialtechnik Dresden – Hochtechnologie für jeden Bereich
Spezialtechnik Dresden – High technology for every sector

Die Spezialtechnik Dresden GmbH gehört zur weltweit tätigen General Atomics Gruppe und steht selber an der Spitze der Spezialtechnik-Gruppe Dresden. Unter ihrem Dach sind Unternehmen aus den unterschiedlichsten Bereichen der Hochtechnologiebranche zusammengeschlossen.
Am Standort Dresden befindet sich neben der Spezialtechnik Dresden GmbH auch die Umwelt- und Ingenieurtechnik GmbH Dresden. Sie bietet maßgeschneiderte Lösungen zur Umwelt- und Landesüberwachung mittels regionaler hydrologischer und radiologischer Messnetze sowie Systeme auf dem Gebiet Wassertechnologie.
Ebenfalls in Dresden ansässig ist die Spezialtechnik Dresden Service GmbH. Sie bewirtschaftet die Immobilien der zur Spezialtechnik-Gruppe gehörenden Unternehmen und vermittelt hochwertige Mietobjekte an interessierte Kunden.
Weitere Schwerpunkte der in der Gruppe zusammengeschlossenen Unternehmen sind die umweltgerechte Verwertung und Entsorgung von Explosivstoffen und Munition, der Tief- und Wasserbau sowie die Rekultivierung von Industrieanlagen und -flächen. Darüber hinaus gehören die Modernisierung und Instandhaltung schienengebundener Spezialfahrzeuge zum Leistungsspektrum der Spezialtechnik-Gruppe Dresden.

The Spezialtechnik Dresden GmbH belongs to the worldwide operative General Atomics Group and stands at the head of the Spezialtechnik Group Dresden. Companies from the most diverse high technology sectors are combined under their umbrella.

In addition to the Spezialtechnik Dresden GmbH, the Umwelt- und Ingenieurtechnik GmbH Dresden is also located in Dresden. It offers tailor-made solutions for environmental monitoring by means of regional hydrological and radiological monitoring networks as well as systems in the area of water technology.
The Spezialtechnik Dresden Service GmbH is located in Dresden too. The company manages real estate belonging to the Spezialtechnik Group of companies and offers premium rental properties to interested clients.

Further focal points of the combined group of companies are environmentally friendly utilization and disposal of explosives and munitions, civil and hydrological engineering as well as the re-cultivation of industrial plants and areas. Over and above this, the modernization and maintenance of rail-bound special vehicles also belong to the range of services offered by the Spezialtechnik Group Dresden.

Spezialtechnik Dresden GmbH

Geschäftsführer/Managing Directors:
Karsten Blue
Linden Blue
Dr. Rainer Eichhorn
Dr. Wolfgang Petzold

Gründungsjahr/Year of foundation:
1990

Mitarbeiter/Employees:
600

Umsatz/Turnover:
65 Millionen Euro
65 million euros

Geschäftstätigkeit/Business activity:
Umwelt- und Bauleistungen, Munitionsentsorgung, Schienenfahrzeuge
Environmental and construction work, munitions disposal, railed vehicles

Anschrift/Address:
Zum Windkanal 21
D-01109 Dresden
Telefon +49 (0) 351 886-5000
Telefax +49 (0) 351 886-5443
info@spezialtechnik.de
www.spezialtechnik.de

Oben: Spezialleistungen im Bau und Umweltsektor.
Above: Special services in the construction and environmental sector.

Unten: Modernisierung und Instandhaltung schienengebundener Spezialfahrzeuge.
Below: Modernization and maintenance of rail-bound special vehicles.

Hohes Niveau an wirtschaftlichen Verflechtungen im Dreiländereck
High level of economic integration at the border triangle

Dr. Detlef Hamann

Der 1956 gebürtige Magdeburger hat in Leipzig Ökonomie studiert und wurde 1986 an der Hochschule für Verkehrswesen Dresden promoviert. Beruflich begann er als wissenschaftlicher Assistent an der Hochschule für Verkehrswesen Dresden, wechselte aber 1988 zur Dresdner Elektromaschinenfirma VEM. Seit 1998 wirkt er für die IHK Dresden, deren Hauptgeschäftsführer er seit 2003 ist.

The author was born in Magdeburg in 1956 and studied economics in Leipzig. He obtained his doctorate at the Dresden University for Transport and Communications in 1986. He started his career as a research assistant, but in 1988 he switched to the Dresden electric machine company, VEM. Since 2003 Dr. Hamann has been CEO at the Dresden Chamber of Industry and Commerce (IHK).

Der französische Schriftsteller Paul Lacroix verglich einmal die Idee, Europa einen zu wollen, mit dem Versuch, ein Omelett zu backen, ohne Eier zu zerschlagen. Das Erstaunliche daran ist, dass Lacroix dieses Bild bereits vor mehr als 170 Jahren prägte. Blicken wir heute auf noch nicht einmal 20 Jahre grenzüberschreitende Zusammenarbeit im Dreiländereck von Sachsen, Tschechien und Polen zurück, scheint es fast so, als tickten die Uhren dort anders – nämlich schneller. Denn es ist ohne Frage beeindruckend, wie viele gemeinsame Projekte im Grenzraum zwischen Deutschland, Polen und Tschechien in vergleichsweise kurzer Zeit realisiert werden konnten. Vielleicht lässt es sich ja – trotz der lange Zeit vorherrschenden ökonomischen, sozialen und gesellschaftlichen Unterschiede – auf ein Fundament, das als Wirtschaftsdreieck Sachsen-Böhmen-Schlesien einmal zu den stärksten und dynamischsten Regionen Europas zählte, heute besser aufbauen als anderswo. Zumindest verdeutlicht die positive Entwicklung der letzten knapp zwei Jahrzehnte, wie stark die Bindungen zwischen den Lebensräumen der Menschen beiderseits der Grenzen immer noch sind. Ein starkes Argument auch für noch Kommendes.

Bedingt durch die geografische Lage Sachsens wird die Entwicklung des Freistaates selbst mehr denn je durch Prozesse jenseits der rund 570 Kilometer langen Staatsgrenze beeinflusst. Betrachtet man die regionale Verteilung der Wohnbevölkerung Sachsens, ist festzustellen, dass in den grenznahen Gebieten rund ein Drittel davon lebt. Darüber hinaus macht die Grenzregion sogar annähernd die Hälfte der sächsischen Landesfläche aus. Nach der EU-Erweiterung am 1. Mai 2004 ist der Stellenwert der grenzüberschreitenden Zusammenarbeit mit Tschechien und Polen für Sachsen erwartungsgemäß noch einmal angestiegen und fand so auch Eingang in den Landesentwicklungsplan des Freistaates. Sachsen hat darin Ziele zur Entwicklung von grenzübergreifenden Kooperationen, für gemeinsame grenzüberschreitende regionale Raumordnungspläne und die Erstellung und Umsetzung gemeinsamer Konzepte definiert, ohne dabei die kulturelle Vielfalt des europäischen Raumes und die Chancen aller Beteiligten zu beschneiden. Diesen Planungen folgend, wurde in der letzten EU-Strukturfondsförderperiode von 2000 bis 2006 auch ein erheblicher Teil der auf Sachsen entfallenden Mittel für die Entwicklung dieser Grenzregion eingesetzt.

Für die Entwicklung grenzüberschreitender Kooperationen und den Ausbau nachbarschaftlicher Beziehungen wird Sachsen jedoch schon deutlich länger die Hilfe der EU zuteil.

Internationality

Hauptgeschäftsstelle der Industrie- und Handelskammer Dresden.
Headquarters of the Dresden Chamber of Industry and Commerce (IHK Dresden).

The French author Paul Lacroix once compared the idea of intending to unify Europe with an attempt at making an omelette without beating eggs. What is astonishing is that Lacroix already formed this view more than 170 years ago. If we today look back at not yet 20 years of transnational collaboration in the border triangle of Saxony, the Czech Republic and Poland, it almost appears that the clocks tick differently there, namely faster. For it is, without a doubt, impressive how many joint projects could be implemented between Germany, Poland and the Czech Republic in the border region in a comparatively short time. Perhaps today you can build on a foundation, which as the economic triangle Saxony-Bohemia-Silesia once counted amongst the strongest and most dynamic regions of Europe, easier than elsewhere – despite the long prevailing economic, social and corporate differences. At least the positive development of the past just under two decades clarifies how strong the connections between the people of the living spaces on both sides of the border still are. A strong argument for that which is still to come.

As a consequence of Saxony's geographical position, the development of the Free State itself is now more than ever influenced through processes beyond the almost 570-kilometre-long state border. If one considers the regional distribution of the resident population of Saxony, it is established that about one third thereof live in the regions close to the border. Furthermore the border region actually accounts for almost half the surface area of Saxony. After the EU expansion on 1 May 2004, the significance of transnational collaboration with the Czech Republic and Poland for Saxony expectedly increased again, and thus also found access to the rural development of the Free State. Therein Saxony has defined goals for the development of transnational co-operations for joint cross-border regional development plans and the preparation and implementation of joint concepts, without in doing so curtailing the cultural diversity of the European zone and the opportunities of all the participants. Thus in the recent EU structural funding period from 2000 to 2006, consequent to these plans, a significant portion of funding allocated to Saxony was also deployed for the development of this border region.

Internationalität

Bereits seit Anfang der 90er Jahre unterstützt die Europäische Union im Rahmen der EU-Gemeinschaftsinitiative INTERREG vielfältige Vorhaben, die die gemeinsamen Grenzgebiete zu einem zukunftsfähigen Wirtschafts- und Lebensraum weiterentwickeln sowie die Wettbewerbsfähigkeit des sächsisch-tschechischen und sächsisch-niederschlesischen Grenzraumes steigern sollen. Mit dem Programm INTERREG III A findet diese Entwicklung in der Förderperiode 2007–2013 ihre Fortsetzung als eigenständiges Ziel mit dem Titel „Europäische territoriale Zusammenarbeit – grenzübergreifende Zusammenarbeit" sowie im „Operationellen Programm der grenzübergreifenden Zusammenarbeit Sachsen · Tschechien · Polen 2007–2013". Die dabei gewährte Projektförderung stellt hohe Anforderungen an die Qualität der Kooperation zwischen den Partnern auf beiden Seiten der Grenzen, um tatsächlich eine nachhaltige territoriale Entwicklung zu gestalten und umzusetzen.

Für die Arbeit der Industrie- und Handelskammer Dresden, deren Kammerbezirk sich in direkter Nachbarschaft zu Polen und Tschechien befindet, im Osten mit einer Länge von 112 Kilometern an die polnischen Wojewodschaften Dolnoslaskie (Niederschlesien) und Lubuskie (Lebus) grenzt sowie im Süden mit einer Grenzlinie von 205 Kilometern zu Tschechien und dem Bezirk Nordböhmen, hat diese spezifische Lage natürlich auch gravierende Auswirkungen.

Internationale Kooperation:
Vertreter der IHK Dresden und der tschechischen Kreiswirtschaftskammer Usti nad Labem unterzeichneten 2007 eine Kooperationsvereinbarung.
International cooperation:
Representatives of the IHK Dresden and the Czech district economic chamber Usti and Labem signed a cooperation agreement in 2007.

For the development of cross-border cooperation and the extension of neighbourly relationships Saxony has however, already for a long period received EU aid. Already since the beginning of the 1990s, the European Union has supported diverse projects, within the scope of the EU community initiative INTERREG, which further develops the common border zones to a sustainable economic and living environment as well as enhances the competitiveness of the Saxony-Czech and Saxony-Lower Silesia border regions. With the INTERREG III A programme, this development finds its continuation in the funding period 2007–2013 as an independent objective with the title "European territorial collaboration – cross-border collaboration" as well as in the "Operational Programme of the cross-border collaboration Saxony · Czechia · Poland 2007–2013". The project funding granted therewith sets great demands on the quality of the cooperation between the partners on both sides of the border to actually design and implement sustainable territorial development.

This specific situation also naturally has grave consequences for the tasks of the Dresden Chamber of Industry and Commerce, whose chamber district is found in the direct neighbourhood of Poland and the Czech Republic, in the east bordering on the Polish Voivodships Dolnoslaskie (Lower Silesia) and Lubuskie (Lebus) with a length of 112 kilometres as well as in the south with a length of 205 kilometres bordering on the Czech Republic and the North Bohemian county.

Despite the fact that the multitude of businesses which have settled here only originated in their present form in the years following German reunification, the traditional economic ties between Saxony, Bohemia and Lower Silesia are still found here and have been revived by co-operation, service and marketing relationships.

Which formidable standards have already been met is already made clear by looking at the foreign trade statistics of Saxony. Under the top target regions of products and services from the Free State, Poland in 2008 ranked a brilliant second with almost 1.5 billion euros, solely outflanked by the USA. The Czech Republic after all came in at a remarkable seventh place with 1.2 billion. The southern neighbour in turn ranked right in front with 2.7 billion euros with the Saxony importations in the previous year: From Poland, products and services to the value of 1.3 billion euros were bought, which meant place three.

With their contact centres for Saxon-Czech economic cooperation in Dresden and Zittau as well as for the Saxon-Polish relationship in Görlitz, the Chamber has been initiating solid practical transnational economic promotion for many years, whether through the disclosure of variegated information, the holding of events, or the imparting of individual business contacts and the organization of bi- or tri-national projects.

Internationalität

Grenzen überschreiten: Austausch der Wirtschaft im Dreiländereck Sachsen/Polen/Tschechien.
Transcending borders: interchange of business in the Saxony/Poland/Czech Republic border triangle.

Trotz der Tatsache, dass die Vielzahl der hier ansässigen Betriebe in ihrer heutigen Form erst in den Nachwendejahren entstanden ist, finden sich nach wie vor traditionelle wirtschaftliche Verflechtungen zwischen Sachsen, Böhmen und Niederschlesien, denen heute durch Kooperations-, Dienstleistungs- und Absatzbeziehungen neues Leben eingehaucht wurde. Welches beachtliche Niveau bereits erreicht wurde, macht allein schon ein Blick auf die sächsische Außenhandelsstatistik deutlich. Unter den Top-Zielregionen von Produkten und Leistungen aus dem Freistaat rangierte Polen 2008 mit fast 1,5 Milliarden Euro, lediglich überflügelt von den USA, auf einem hervorragenden zweiten Rang, Tschechien kam mit rund 1,2 Milliarden immerhin noch auf einen beachtlichen Platz sieben. Ganz vorn rangiert der südliche Nachbar dafür mit 2,7 Milliarden Euro im vergangenen Jahr bei den sächsischen Importen, aus Polen wurden Waren und Leistungen im Wert von 1,3 Milliarden Euro eingekauft, was Rang drei bedeutete.

Mit ihren Kontaktzentren für sächsisch-tschechische Wirtschaftskooperation in Dresden und Zittau sowie für sächsisch-polnische Beziehungen in Görlitz initiiert die Kammer seit vielen Jahren ganz praktische grenzüberschreitende Wirtschaftsförderung, durch die Gewährung vielfältiger Auskünfte, die Durchführung von Veranstaltungen, oder die Vermittlung einzelbetrieblicher Kontakte und die Organisation bi- oder trinationaler Projekte.

Dass dieses Engagement Wirkung zeigt, haben die regionalen Unternehmen bereits mehrfach attestiert. Bisher sind vor allem Firmen des produzierenden Gewerbes und des Handels in den Genuss grenzüberschreitender Geschäftsvorteile gekommen. Reale Distanzen – von allen Orten des Kammerbezirks in die angrenzenden Nachbarländer – stellen dabei nach Auskunft vieler Betriebe kein echtes Hindernis dar. Am ehesten setzt hier die vorhandene Straßeninfrastruktur noch Grenzen. In Zukunft werden mit großer Sicherheit noch weitere Branchen zu den Profiteuren beiderseits der Grenzen gehören, denn die Region zwischen Sachsen, Polen und Tschechien wird sich weiter angleichen und zu noch größeren wirtschaftlichen Verflechtungen gelangen.

Mit diesem fortschreitenden Prozess wird sich aber auch der Wettbewerbsdruck auf alle Unternehmen des trinationalen Wirtschaftsraumes erhöhen. Für unsere sächsischen Firmen könnte dies durchaus größere Herausforderungen mit sich bringen als für tschechische und polnische, welche ihre neue Positionierung zwischen billiger oder technologisch hochwertiger, aber kostenintensiverer Produktion noch suchen. Die intensive Nutzung der bestehenden IHK-Kontaktzentren für Wirtschaftskooperation, die Umsetzung der Kooperationsvereinbarungen der sächsischen Kammern mit denen in den Nachbarländern, grenzüberschreitende Projekte von Verbänden, Unternehmensnetzwerken und Technologiezentren können und müssen diesen Prozess daher aktiv und wegweisend begleiten.

Trotz des schon Erreichten und des ab und zu durchaus auch verdienten Innehaltens und Zurückblickens muss es gelten, weiter nach vorn zu schauen, sich weiter zu verbessern und neue Potenziale zu erschließen. Denn letztlich lassen sich die drei aneinander grenzenden Länder und die EU die Entwicklung dieser Grenzregionen nicht ohne Grund einiges kosten.

Wie die Zukunft genau aussehen wird, weiß niemand, konkrete Vorstellungen und Erwartungen existieren aber sehr wohl. So, dass die Euroregion noch mehr als eine gemeinsame Region erkannt und sich gleichermaßen attraktiv für Unternehmer wie für Arbeitnehmerinnen und Arbeitnehmer darstellen und entwickeln wird. Nicht abstrakte Diskussionen über die Konkurrenz um den niedrigsten Lohn und die höchsten Subventionen dürfen die bestimmenden Themen sein, sondern die Ausstrahlung als Entwicklungsregion mit vielfältigen Potenzialen. Dafür müssen zusätzliche Initiativen entwickelt werden, die wiederum Impulse auslösen können.

Internationality

That this commitment is making an impact has already been attested repeatedly by the regional organizations. So far, especially firms in the producing and mercantile trade could profit of cross-border business advantages. Practical distances – from all locations of the chamber district to the bordering neighbouring countries – represent no real obstacle, according to the information received from many organizations. Most likely the existing road infrastructure still presents barriers here. In future even more industries will most certainly belong to the profiteers on both sides of the border, as the region between Saxony, Poland and the Czech Republic aligns itself and reaches even greater economic integration.

With this progressive process, however, the competitive pressure on all the organizations in the tri-nation economic zone will also increase. For our Saxon firms, this could well bring greater challenges than for the Polish and Czech ones, which are still searching their position between cheaper or technological high-grade, but more cost-effective production. The intensive utilization of the available IHK (Chamber of Industry and Commerce) contact centres for economic cooperation, the realization of cooperation agreements of the Saxon chambers with those of the neighbouring countries, trans-national association projects, organizational networks and technology centres can and must actively and seminally accompany this process.

Despite the already achieved and at times also well-deserved pauses and reflecting, it must in force continuing to look ahead, to continue improving and to develop new potential. For ultimately, the three bordering countries and the EU will not without reason allow the significant costs of the development of theses border regions.

What exactly the future will bring, nobody knows, solid notions and expectations however no doubt exist. For instance, that the Euro region will be even more recognized as a collective region and likewise represent and develop to be attractive for entrepreneurs as much as for employees. The decisive topics may not be abstract discussions relating to competitors and the lowest wage and the highest subsidy, but rather the vibrancy of a development region with manifold potential. Therefore additional initiatives must be developed, which can in turn release momentum.

Dresden, Sachsen, Mitteldeutschland – Regionale Kooperation als Wettbewerbsvorteil
Dresden, Saxony, Middle Germany – Regional cooperation as competitive advantage

Klaus Wurpts M.A.
Der Autor ist seit 2005 Geschäftsführer der Wirtschaftsinitiative für Mitteldeutschland GmbH. Der gebürtige Niedersachse hat Politikwissenschaft in Paris und Leipzig studiert und als wissenschaftlicher Mitarbeiter an verschiedenen Instituten sowie als freier Publizist gearbeitet. Ab 2003 war er Projektleiter für den länderübergreifenden Clusterprozess beim ehemaligen Regionenmarketing Mitteldeutschland.

The author has been the managing director of the Industrial Initiative for Central Germany since 2005. He was born in Lower Saxony and studied political science in Paris and Leipzig. He worked as a scientific officer at various institutions as well as being a journalist. From 2003, he was a project manager for the cross-national cluster process at the former Regionenmarketing Mitteldeutschland.

Regionale Kooperation gilt bei Wirtschaftsexperten als ein wichtiger Standortvorteil. Wenn Unternehmen „über den eigenen Tellerrand hinausschauen" und mit anderen Unternehmen oder Forschungseinrichtungen in der Umgebung zusammenarbeiten, können sie durch Kostensenkung und Spezialisierung besondere Wettbewerbsvorteile am Markt erzielen.

Für viele Unternehmen in Dresden erstreckt sich diese Kooperation nicht nur auf die eigene Stadt. In zahlreichen Zulieferer- und Kooperationsverhältnissen profitieren sie von einer regionalen Einbindung über die sächsischen Ländergrenzen hinaus bis weit hinein nach Sachsen-Anhalt und Thüringen. Die regionale Vernetzung in Mitteldeutschland trägt dabei nicht nur zu einem verstärkten wirtschaftlichen Wachstum „aus eigener Kraft" bei, sondern bietet auch neuen Investoren ein attraktives Umfeld und strahlt entsprechend aus. Deshalb wird dieser Prozess sowohl durch die Politik mit der „Initiative Mitteldeutschland" der Ministerpräsidenten als auch durch die von Unternehmen getragene, bundesweit einmalige Wirtschaftsinitiative für Mitteldeutschland aktiv gefördert. Denn, so lautet das Motto der Wirtschaftsinitiative: Wenn es den Unternehmen gut geht, geht es auch der Region gut, und umgekehrt. Dabei kennt Wirtschaft keine Ländergrenzen.

Die wohl prominentesten Beispiele für länderübergreifende Kooperationen sind die Automobil- und die Photovoltaik Industrie. Daneben gibt es auch in Bereichen wie der Informationstechnologie oder der Biotechnologie zahlreiche Verbindungen Dresdner Unternehmen und Forschungseinrichtungen mit Partnern bis hin zu den gut angebundenen mitteldeutschen Zentren in Leipzig, Erfurt und Magdeburg.

Der Automobilstandort Dresden ist gemeinhin durch die Gläserne Manufaktur von Volkswagen bekannt. Außer einigen Zulieferern und Automotive-nahen Maschinenbauern konnte sich hier zudem die Technische Universität (TU) Dresden, insbesondere mit den Instituten für Automobiltechnik, für Fahrzeugtechnik sowie für Leichtbau und Kunststofftechnik, besonders profilieren. Die regionale Integration erstreckt sich über das sächsische Automobilzulieferernetzwerk AMZ in alle Teile Ostdeutschlands. Auf Bestreben der Unternehmen hat sich entsprechend das „Automotive Cluster Ostdeutschland" (ACOD) gegründet. Dieses verbindet den Automobilstandort Dresden auch mit den OEM-Werken von Daimler in Ludwigsfelde oder Opel in Eisenach. Das Spektrum der Aktivitäten umfasst gemeinsame Forschungs- und Entwicklungsleistungen, gemeinsame themenzentrierte Workshops wie auch vielfältige Marketingaktivitäten.

Networking

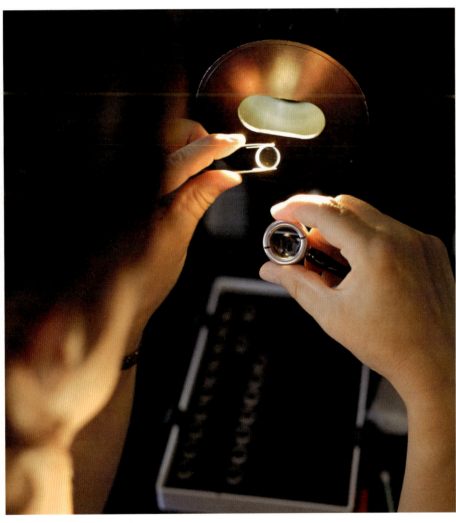

Linsen von Carl Zeiss Jena.
Lenses by Carl Zeiss Jena.

Regional cooperation is considered an important location advantage by economic experts. When organizations "look beyond their own noses" and collaborate with other organizations or research institutions in the vicinity, they can, by way of cost reductions and specialization, achieve specific competitive advantages in the market.

For many organizations in Dresden this cooperation does not only stretch across its own city borders. In numerous supplier- and cooperation relations they profit from a regional involvement over the Saxony state borders and beyond, far away into Saxony-Anhalt and Thuringia. The regional networking in Middle Germany not only contributes towards a stronger economic growth "on its own strength", however also offers new investors an attractive environment and radiates accordingly. Hence, this process is actively promoted by politics with the "Initiative Mitteldeutschland" (Middle Germany Initiative) of the Prime Ministers, as also by the nationwide unique Industrial Initiative for Central Germany, which is supported by the organizations. For, this is the motto of the economic initiative: If the organizations are doing well, the region also does well and vice versa. The economy knows no state boundaries.

The perhaps most prominent examples of cross-national cooperation are the automotive and photovoltaic industry. In addition, there are also numerous networks in areas such as information technology or biotechnology, of the Dresden organizations and research institutions with partners, right up to the well-connected Middle German centres in Leipzig, Erfurt and Magdeburg.

The Dresden automotive location is generally known by Volkswagen's glass manufacture. Besides several suppliers and automotive-related mechanical engineering companies, the Dresden University of Technology (TU Dresden) could additionally distinguish itself here, in particular with the institutions for automotive technology, for vehicle technology as well as for lightweight construction and plastics technology. Regional integration stretches across the Saxony Automotive Supplier Network (AMZ) into all parts of Eastern Germany. Upon the aspiration of organizations, the "Automotive Cluster Ostdeutschland" (ACOD), was accordingly founded.

Vernetzung

Ähnlich ist es in der Photovoltaik-industrie, die nicht nur für Dresden und Umgebung eine wichtige Zukunftstechnologie darstellt. Hier hat sich ganz Mitteldeutschland zu einer der weltweit führenden Photovoltaik-Regionen entwickelt. 90 Prozent der in Deutschland produzierten Solarzellen kommen von hier, das macht fast 20 Prozent Weltmarktanteil. In einigen Segmenten zählen Unternehmen aus Mitteldeutschland zu den Marktführern. Wie viele Standorte in Mitteldeutschland, hat die Wirtschaftsregion Dresden hier einen ganz besonderen Wettbewerbsvorteil. Neben der hervorragenden Infrastruktur und den hohen Fördermöglichkeiten stehen vor allem zahlreiche hoch qualifizierte Fachkräfte zur Verfügung. Grund dafür ist die zunehmende Verzahnung der Solarbranche mit der seit Jahrzehnten aufgebauten Mikroelektronik. Das von 30 Firmen, zehn Forschungseinrichtungen und vier Hochschulen aus Sachsen, Sachsen-Anhalt und Thüringen initiierte „Solarvalley Mitteldeutschland" wurde vom Bundesforschungsministerium als nationales „Spitzencluster" ausgezeichnet und arbeitet mit umfangreichen Forschungsgeldern nun daran, bis zum Jahr 2015 die Kosten für die Herstellung von Solarstrom auf den Preis herkömmlicher Energieträger zu senken.
Beispielhaft wurden die länderübergreifenden Clusterbildungsprozesse von den drei Landesverwaltungen in Sachsen, Sachsen-Anhalt und Thüringen unterstützt. Die förderseitige Abstimmung umfasste sogar die Ausreichung von Mitteln für Aktivitäten über das jeweils eigene Bundesland hinaus – eine bemerkenswerte Seltenheit im deutschen Wettbewerbsföderalismus, die jedoch den erreichten regionalen Kooperationsstatus verdeutlicht. „Wachstumsbranchen stärken" lautet entsprechend eines der Ziele der auch maßgeblich aus Dresden angeschobenen politischen „Initiative Mitteldeutschland". Neben zahlreichen Kooperationsvorhaben auf Verwaltungsebene hat sich die Politik der drei Länder weitere ambitionierte Ziele für die Zusammenarbeit gegeben: So sollen „optimale Bedingungen für Investitionen und unternehmerische Initiativen" geschaffen sowie Forschungs- und Innovationspotenziale gemeinsam ausgebaut und vernetzt werden.

Den länderübergreifenden „mitteldeutschen Gedanken" unterstützen auch zahlreiche Unternehmen aus den drei Bundesländern mit dem Verein „Wirtschaftsinitiative für Mitteldeutschland", der sich im Zusammenspiel mit Städten und Kammern als „Aktionsplattform strukturbestimmender Unternehmen" zur „Entwicklung und Vermarktung der traditionsreichen Wirtschaftsregion Mitteldeutschland" versteht. Die bereits über 60 Mitglieder der im Jahr 2000 gegründeten Initiative fördern die länderübergreifende Cluster- und Netzwerkbildung mit eigenen Finanzmitteln und Managementkapazitäten, sie unterstützen zukunftsträchtige Innovationsprojekte und tragen mit der als regionale Leitmesse konzipierten „Absolventenmesse Mitteldeutschland" zur Sicherung des regionalen Fachkräftebedarfs bei.

Neben der bereits erreichten wirtschaftlichen Integration in Mitteldeutschland bahnt sich derzeit auch eine mitteldeutsche Zusammenarbeit auf kommunaler Ebene an. Die Perspektive einer künftig an so genannten „Metropolregionen" ausgerichteten Förderpolitik der Europäische Union (EU) lässt – analog zu den Unternehmen und Forschungseinrichtungen – auch die größten Kommunen aus Mitteldeutschland enger kooperieren. Für viele stellt dieses gar eine der wichtigen Weichenstellungen für die Zukunft des Wirtschaftsstandorts dar.

Networking

Thüringen, Sachsen-Anhalt und Sachsen streben eine länderübergreifende Zusammenarbeit an.
Thuringia, Saxony-Anhalt and Saxony strive towards a cross-national cooperation.

(v.l./l. to r.) Dr. Manfred Gieseler
(Ex-Aufsichtsratsvorsitzender/
Ex-Chairman of the Supervisory Board),
Klaus Wurpts
(Geschäftsführer/Managing Director),
Prof. Dr. Georg Frank
(1. Vorsitzender/Chairman of the Board).

This also connects the Dresden automotive location with the OEM works of Daimler in Ludwigsfelde or Opel in Eisenach. The range of activities encompasses joint research and development accomplishments, joint topic-centred workshops as well as varied marketing activities.

It is similar in the photovoltaic industry, which not only represents an important future technology for Dresden and its surroundings. Here, the entire Middle Germany has developed itself into one of the leading photovoltaic regions in the world. 90 per cent of solar cells produced in Germany come from here, which amounts to almost 20 per cent of the global market share. In several segments, the organizations in Middle Germany are counted amongst the market leaders. Like many locations in Middle Germany, the Dresden economic region has a very specific competitive edge here. Besides the excellent infrastructure and the great support measures, there are in particular many highly qualified employees available. The reason for this is the ever-increasing interlocking of the solar industry with the microelectronic industry, which was established decades ago. The "Solarvalley Mitteldeutschland" – initiated by 30 firms, ten research institutions and four universities from Saxony, Saxony-Anhalt and Thuringia – was distinguished by the Federal Research Ministry as the national "top cluster" and with numerous research funds is now until 2015 working on reducing the costs of producing solar energy down to the price of conventional energy sources.

The cross-national cluster building processes are being supported by the three state authorities of Saxony, Saxony-Anhalt and Thuringia in an exemplary manner. The coordination from the promoters' side even comprised the granting of funding for activities which extend beyond the respective own state – a remarkable rarity in German competitive federalism, which nevertheless clarifies the achieved regional cooperation status. "Strengthen growth industries" is accordingly one of the objectives of the political "Middle Germany Initiative", which is also decisively pushed forward from Dresden. In addition to numerous cooperation projects on administrative level, the policies of the three states have given further ambitious objectives for collaboration: In this way, "optimal conditions for investments and entrepreneurial initiatives" should be created as well as the joint development and networking of research and innovation potential.

Numerous organizations of the three states also support cross-national "Middle German thinking" through the "Industrial Initiative for Central Germany" association, which in collaboration with cities and chambers, considers itself the "action platform for structure-determining organizations" for the "development and marketing of the long-established Middle German economic region". The already more than 60 members of the initiative, which was founded in 2000, promote cross-national cluster and network building through internal financing and management capacities, they support promising innovation projects and contribute towards the security of regional qualified employee demand with the "Absolventenmesse Mitteldeutschland" (alumni trade show), designed as the leading trade show.

In addition to the already achieved economic integration in Middle Germany, a current Middle German collaboration is being channelled on a municipal level. The prospect of a future European Union (EU) funding policy aligned in so-called "metropolis regions" – modelled on the organizations and research institutions – also provide for close cooperation between the largest municipalities in Middle Germany. For many, this even represents one of the important decisions for the future of the economic region.

Company Profile

Berufsakademie Sachsen

Direktorenkonferenz/Board of Directors:
Prof. Dr. Detlef Kröppelin
(Vorsitzender/Chairman)

Prof. Heinz Zieger
(stellvertretender Vorsitzender/Deputy Chairman)

Gründungsjahr/Year of foundation:
1991

Standorte/Locations:
Bautzen
www.ba-bautzen.de
Breitenbrunn
www.ba-breitenbrunn.de
Dresden
www.ba-dresden.de
Glauchau
www.ba-glauchau.de
Leipzig
www.ba-leipzig.de
Plauen
www.ba-plauen.de
Riesa
www.ba-riesa.de

Geschäftstätigkeit/Business activity:
Duales Studium in den Bereichen Informatik, Technik, Wirtschaft und Sozialwesen in zurzeit insgesamt 51 Studiengängen
Dual theoretical and practical studies in Technology, Information Science, Commerce and Social Science in currently 51 degree programmes

Anschrift/Address:
Heideparkstraße 8
D-01099 Dresden
Telefon +49 (0) 351 81334-0
Telefax +49 (0) 351 81334-29
info@ba-dresden.de
www.ba-dresden.de

Berufsakademie Sachsen – Eine zukunftsfähige duale Studienform
University of Cooperative Education – Future-oriented dual education

Die Berufsakademie (BA) Sachsen wurde nach dem Baden-Württembergischen Modell am 1. Oktober 1991 gegründet und umfasst sieben Studienakademien mit den Standorten Bautzen, Breitenbrunn, Dresden, Glauchau, Leipzig, Plauen und Riesa. Mit diesem Schritt wurde das duale Ausbildungsprinzip in den tertiären Bereich und damit in die sächsische Hochschullandschaft integriert.

Anders als an den Fachhochschulen und Universitäten werden die Studenten in einem zwölfwöchigen Wechsel in drei Jahren sowohl in Theorie als auch Praxis ausgebildet. Dabei sind die Ausbildungsbetriebe gleichberechtigte Partner der akademischen Ausbildung.

Die Berufsakademie bietet in den Bereichen Informatik, Technik, Wirtschaft und Sozialwesen zur Zeit insgesamt 51 Studiengänge an. Die Studienabschlüsse sind denen der Fachhochschulen gleichgestellt und werden europaweit anerkannt. Bis spätestens 2010 werden alle sieben Studienakademien von Diplom- auf Bachelor-Studiengänge umstellen.

Durch den starken Praxisbezug ist das BA-Studium eine attraktive Alternative zur Hochschule, zumal das Studium kurz und intensiv ist und die Arbeitsmarktchance nach dem Studium je nach Studiengang bis zu 90 Prozent beträgt. Der Grund: Hier wird direkt nach dem Bedarf der Wirtschaft ausgebildet.

The Berufsakademie "BA" Sachsen was founded on 1 October 1991 based on the Baden-Württemberg model and comprises seven academies in Bautzen, Breitenbrunn, Dresden, Glauchau, Leipzig, Plauen and Riesa. In this way the principle of dual vocational training was transferred to the level of tertiary education in Saxony.

In contrast to universities of applied sciences and universities, the students receive both theoretical and practical training in alternating twelve-week blocks over a period of three years. This means that the companies are equal partners in the world of academic education. The university of cooperative education are currently offering a total of 51 courses in Information Science, Technology, Commerce and Social Science. The degrees are equivalent to those offered by universities of applied sciences and are recognized throughout Europe. All of the seven academies will convert their traditional degree courses to internationally comparable "Bachelor" courses until 2010 at the latest. Due to a strong focus on practical experience, studies at Berufsakademie are an attractive alternative to a course offered by a university, particularly since the courses are short and intensive. Furthermore, the chance to find a job after graduation are – depending on the type of course – as high as up to 90 per cent.

Company Profile

Modern und marktgerecht – Studienangebote auf höchstem Niveau
Modern and market-driven – Study courses of the highest standard

Die im Jahr 2003 auf Initiative der Technischen Universität Dresden gegründete Dresden International University (DIU) ist eine moderne, berufsnahe Netzwerkeinrichtung, die unter dem Dach der TUDAG mit ausgewähltem Lehrpersonal aus Hochschulprofessoren, Dozenten und Führungskräften der Praxis berufsbegleitende oder berufsunterbrechende Weiterbildungsprogramme anbietet. Die Programme sind interdisziplinär konzipiert und entweder als Bachelor- beziehungsweise Master-Studiengänge oder Zertifikatskurse angelegt. Sie erreichten in bislang 16 verschiedenen Studiengängen mehr als 400 aktuell eingeschriebene deutsche und ausländische Studierende.

Schwerpunktthemen kommen in Lehre und Forschung aus dem Gesundheitswesen und speziellen medizinischen Entwicklungen. Eine Besonderheit sind Weiterbildungs- und Behandlungsangebote der Traditionellen Chinesischen Medizin. Aber auch Themen aus den Ingenieur-, Wirtschafts- und Kulturwissenschaften werden kontinuierlich angeboten.

Die Ausbildung ist individuell, dienstleistungsorientiert und auf die parallele Berufstätigkeit der Teilnehmer abgestimmt. Die Graduierungsarbeiten werden von berufenen Professoren betreut und bewertet.

The Dresden International University (DIU), which was founded in 2003 on the initiative of the Dresden University of Technology (TUD), is a modern, practice-oriented network establishment. The DIU, under the umbrella of the TUDAG Enterprise Group, offers in-service training courses and co-operative further education with selective teaching staff consisting of university professors, lecturers and business executives. The study programmes are interdisciplinarily designed and are either applied as bachelor's degrees and master's degrees or certificate courses, as the case may be. To date they equal more than 400 German and foreign students currently registered in 16 different study courses.

Primary focal points in teaching and research are derived from the health care system and special medical developments. A distinctive feature is the advanced training and treatment offers of Traditional Chinese Medicine. Topics from the engineering, business and cultural sciences are also continually offered.

The study courses are designed for individual learning, service-oriented and aligned parallel to the occupation of the participant. Graduate theses are overseen and appraised by appointed professors.

Dresden International University gGmbH (DIU)

Präsident/President:
Prof. Dr. Achim Mehlhorn

Ehrenpräsident/Honorary President:
Prof. Dr. Kurt Biedenkopf

Geschäftsführer/Manager:
Dr. Reinhard Kretzschmar

Gründungsjahr/Year of foundation: 2003

Geschäftsfelder/Business fields:
Studienprogramme:
Bachelor, Master, duale Ausbildungsmodelle, Zertifikatskurse
Traditionelle Chinesische Medizin:
Weiterbildung; Patientenbehandlung (DIU-TCM-Ambulanz)
Dienstleistungen für sächsische Hochschulen:
Studierenden-Qualifizierung „Ready for the Job", Soft-Skills
Study courses:
Bachelor, master, dual degree models, certificate courses
Traditional Chinese Medicine:
Continuing education; patient care (DIU-TCM-Health Care Centre)
Services for Saxon universities:
student qualification "Ready for the Job", soft skills

Mitarbeiter/Employees: 24

Dozenten/Lecturers: 200

Studenten/Students: 400

Umsatz 2008/Turnover 2008:
3.400.000 Euro/3,400,000 euros

Anschrift/Address:
Chemnitzer Straße 46b
D-01187 Dresden
Telefon +49 (0) 351 463-32326
Telefax +49 (0) 351 463-33956
info@di-uni.de
www.dresden-international-university.de

Links: DIU-Award 2007.
Left: DIU Award 2007.

Rechts: Verabschiedung der Absolventen des Studienganges Wirtschaft und Recht (2003).
Right: Farewell bidding for graduates of the economic and legal science study course (2003).

Dresden bietet exzellente Forschung und beste Hochschulausbildung
Dresden offers excellent research and first-rate tertiary education

Dr. Eva-Maria Stange

Die 1957 geborene Autorin ist Staatsministerin für Wissenschaft und Kunst im Freistaat Sachsen. Die promovierte Mathematik- und Physiklehrerin wurde 1993 Vorsitzende der Gewerkschaft Erziehung und Wissenschaft in Sachsen und 1997 Bundesvorsitzende der GEW. Seit 1998 ist sie außerdem Executive Board Member von Education International und Mitglied verschiedener Universitätskuratorien.

The author was born in 1957 and is the Minister of State for Arts and Science for the Free State of Saxony. The postdoctoral mathematics and physics teacher became the chairperson of the Trade Union for Education and Science (GEW) in Saxony in 1993, and in 1997 she became the federal chairperson of the GEW. Since 1998 she has also been an executive board member of Education International and a member of the board of trustees of numerous universities.

Jeder, der in Dresden einmal die „Lange Nacht der Wissenschaften" miterlebt hat, weiß: Dresden ist eine Stadt der Wissenschaften. Für jedermann wird in dieser Nacht sicht- und erlebbar, wie unglaublich vielseitig die Forschungsthemen sind, mit denen sich die Dresdner Wissenschaftlerinnen und Wissenschaftler beschäftigen. Die „Lange Nacht der Wissenschaften" gibt dem Publikum einen Einblick in die äußerst vielfältige Dresdner Hochschul- und Wissenschaftslandschaft:

Die sächsische Landeshauptstadt wartet mit zehn Hochschulen auf. Über 40.000 Studierende aus 114 Nationen können aus etwa 200 verschiedenen Studiengängen auswählen. Mit rund 33.000 Studentinnen und Studenten ist die Technische Universität Dresden die größte sächsische Universität, sie bietet eine Ausbildung in über 100 Studiengängen. Im Zuge der Bundesexzellenzinitiative hat die TU Dresden mit einem Exzellenzcluster und einer Graduiertenschule zudem ihre Exzellenz bewiesen. Die Hochschule für Technik und Wirtschaft ist mit über 5.000 Studenten die zweitgrößte Hochschule der Stadt. In 33 Studiengängen bietet sie den Studierenden eine Ausbildung in den Bereichen Technik, Gestaltung, Wirtschaft und Umwelt. Wer eine besonders praxisorientierte Ausbildung sucht, ist bei der Berufsakademie gut aufgehoben, einer ihrer sieben Standorte befindet sich in Dresden.

Aber Dresden ist nicht nur eine Stadt der Naturwissenschaftler und Ingenieure. Einzigartige künstlerische Studiengänge bieten die Hochschule für Bildende Künste Dresden, die Hochschule für Musik „Carl Maria von Weber" Dresden oder die berühmte Palucca-Schule Dresden – Hochschule für Tanz.
Die Palucca-Schule ist die einzige eigenständige Hochschule für Tanz in Deutschland. Gegründet 1925 von Gret Palucca, werden hier klassischer und zeitgenössischer Tanz sowie Improvisation gelehrt. Die Hochschule für Bildende Künste gehört zu den ältesten ihrer Art im deutschsprachigen Raum. Sie geht zurück auf die erste, 1680 gestiftete „Zeichen- und Malerschule". Berühmte Maler wie Caspar David Friedrich und Otto Dix lehrten hier. Die Hochschule für Musik steht in der reichen musikalischen Tradition Dresdens.

Weitere fünf Hochschulen sind in freier Trägerschaft: Die Dresden International University, die Evangelische Hochschule für Soziale Arbeit Dresden, die Hochschule für Kirchenmusik, die Fachhochschule für Religionspädagogik und Gemeindediakonie Moritzburg und die Fachhochschule der Sächsischen Verwaltung Meißen.

Education

Die Wahl des Studienortes ist ein wichtiger und spannender Schritt. Dresden bietet neben umfangreichen fachlichen Angeboten auch ein attraktives Freizeit- und Erlebnisangebot.
The choice of a study location is an important and exciting step. In addition to comprehensive qualification propositions, Dresden also offers attractive recreational and adventure activities.

© Gerd Kleinert/PIXELIO

Anyone who has once witnessed the "Lange Nacht der Wissenschaften" (Long Night of Sciences) in Dresden knows: Dresden is a city of sciences. On this night it is possible for everyone to visualize and experience how unbelievably diverse the research topics are with which Dresden scientists are engaged. The "Long Night of Sciences" gives the audience an insight into the extreme diversity of Dresden's academic and scientific community:

The Saxon state capital boasts ten universities. Over 40,000 students from 114 nations are able to choose from about 200 different study courses. With around 33,000 students, the Dresden University of Technology (TU Dresden) is the largest university in Saxony and offers qualifications in more than 100 study courses. The TU Dresden, with its excellence cluster and a graduate school, has furthermore demonstrated its excellence in the course of the "Bundesexzellenzinitiative" (federal excellence initiative). The Dresden University of Applied Sciences is the second largest university in the city with over 5,000 students. It offers students 33 study courses with qualifications in the areas of engineering, design, economics and environmental studies. Someone looking for an especially practice-oriented qualification is in good hands at the University of Cooperative Education, which has one of its seven locations in Dresden.

However, Dresden is not only a city of natural scientists and engineers. Unique artistic study courses are offered by the Dresden University of Visual Arts (HfBK Dresden), the Hochschule für Musik "Carl Maria von Weber" Dresden (University of Music) and the famous Palucca-Schule Dresden – a university of dance.

The Palucca-Schule is the only independent university of dance in Germany. Founded by Gret Palucca in 1925, classical and contemporary dance as well as improvisation is taught here. The University of Visual Arts belongs to the oldest of its kind in the German-language regions. It dates back to the "Zeichen- und Malerschule" (Drawing and Painters School), which was first founded in 1680. Famous painters such as Caspar David Friedrich and Otto Dix taught here. The University of Music is in keeping with the rich musical tradition of Dresden.

Bildung

**Meike Neitz, die an der TU Dresden Internationale Beziehungen studiert, enthüllt gemeinsam mit der Ministerin bei der Auftaktveranstaltung zur Kampagne „Pack dein Studium. Am besten in Sachsen." in Dresden das Plakatmotiv.
Mit der Kampagne sollen noch mehr Abiturienten davon überzeugt werden, dass es sich lohnt, in Sachsen zu studieren.
Meike Neitz, who studies international relations at the TU Dresden, unveils the poster motive with the Minister at the kick-off event in Dresden for the "Pack dein Studium. Am besten in Dresden." campaign.
With the campaign, even more high-school graduates should be convinced that it is worth studying in Saxony.**

Neben einem breiten Studienangebot zählt für die angehenden Akademiker vor allem das attraktive Studienumfeld in Dresden: 32 Studentenwohnheime mit 6.700 Plätzen, vergleichsweise günstige Mieten und ein breites Kultur- und Freizeitangebot sind gute Argumente, um in der sächsischen Landeshauptstadt zu studieren.

Neben einer vielfältigen Hochschullandschaft kann Dresden mit einer starken Forschungslandschaft punkten: Mit elf Einrichtungen ist Dresden heute zum zweitgrößten Standort der Fraunhofer-Gesellschaft in Deutschland aufgerückt. Vier Einrichtungen der Leibniz-Gemeinschaft, drei Max-Planck-Institute sowie zahlreiche An-Institute an den Hochschulen ergänzen die universitäre Forschung. Im nationalen und internationalen Wettbewerb haben sich diese Einrichtungen als anerkannte Forschungsstätten einen Namen gemacht.

Wo die Wissenschaft stark ist, bleibt auch der wirtschaftliche Erfolg nicht aus. Ein besonderes eindrucksvolles Beispiel dafür ist die Biotechnologie. Ein deutliches Zeichen für den Erfolg der sächsischen Biotechnologieoffensive auf dem Gebiet der Wissenschaft ist das Einwerben des ersten Sonderforschungsbereiches zur Stammzellforschung und des Forschungszentrums „Regenerative Therapien" (CRTD) bei der Deutschen Forschungsgemeinschaft. Um diese wissenschaftlichen Leuchttürme herum entwickelt sich mit wachsendem Erfolg und in enger Nachbarschaft eine Vielzahl junger innovativer Biotechnologieunternehmen.

Damit uns der wissenschaftliche Nachwuchs von morgen nicht ausgeht, werben wir gemeinsam mit den sächsischen Hochschulen mit unserer Kampagne „Pack dein Studium. Am besten in Sachsen." um die Studierenden von morgen: um die eigenen Landeskinder ebenso wie um die der anderen Bundesländer. Ziel ist es, möglichst viele junge Menschen für ein Studium zu motivieren, um dem drohenden Fachkräftemangel der nächsten Jahre entgegenzuwirken. Mit dem Hochschulpakt 2020 haben sich Bund und Länder darauf verständigt, bis 2010 deutlich mehr Studienplätze zur Verfügung zu stellen, um dem in den westdeutschen Bundesländern bevorstehenden „Studentenberg" eine attraktive Perspektive zu bieten.

Education 43

Am Ende steht der Erfolg! Sächsische Hochschulabsolventen haben glänzende Berufsaussichten, nicht nur bei regionalen Unternehmen. Deutschlands Hightech-Standort trumpft mit Konzernen wie AMD, EADS, Plastic Logic und mit zahlreichen Forschungsnetzwerken auf. Optimale Karrierechancen für junge Wissenschaftler.
In the end success triumphs! Saxon university graduates have glowing career prospects, not only at regional enterprises. Germany's high-tech location boasts groups such as AMD, EADS, Plastic Logic and numerous research networks. Optimal career opportunities for young academics.

A further five universities operate independently: the Dresden International University, the Evangelische Hochschule für Soziale Arbeit Dresden (evangelic university for social work), the Hochschule für Kirchenmusik (university of church music), the Fachhochschule für Religionspädagogik und Gemeindediakonie Moritzburg (technical university of religious education and parish services) and the Fachhochschule der Sächsischen Verwaltung Meißen (technical university for Saxon administrative affairs).

In addition to a wide selection of study courses, the attractive study environment in Dresden is of particular importance for prospective students. 32 student dormitories, which accommodate 6,700 students, comparatively cheap renting and a wide range of cultural and recreational offers are strong arguments for studying in the Saxon state capital.

Besides a diverse academic landscape, Dresden also scores points with a strong research community: With eleven institutions, Dresden has risen to be the second-largest location of the Fraunhofer Society in Germany today. Four institutions of the Leibniz Scientific community, three Max Planck institutes as well as numerous affiliated university institutions complete the university research. In national and international competition, these institutions have made a name for themselves as acknowledged research locations.

Where science is strong, economic success also follows. A particularly impressive example of this is biotechnology. A clear indication of the success of the Saxon Biotechnology-Offensive in the field of science is the procurement of the first special research area for stem cell research and the Center for Regenerative Therapies Dresden (CRTD) from the German Research Foundation.

Growing success is developing around these scientific beacons, and in close proximity, a multitude of young innovative biotechnology enterprises.

To prevent the young scientific talent of tomorrow from running out, we are canvassing the students of tomorrow with our campaign "Pack dein Studium. Am besten in Sachsen." (Do your degree. At best in Saxony) together with the Saxon universities: aimed at Saxon youth as well as those of other federal states. The objective is to motivate as many young people as possible for a degree course in order to counter the threatening shortage in qualified labour of the next few years. With the Higher Education Pact 2020, the federal government and the federal states have agreed to make significantly more student places available by 2010, so as to offer attractive prospects to the impending "mountain of students" in the West-German states.

Know-how-Transfer in Dresden – Wissen vermarkten, Zukunft gestalten
Know-how transfer in Dresden – Promoting knowledge, shaping the future

Ulrich Assmann

Der Autor wurde 1956 in Osnabrück geboren und studierte in Clausthal und München. Er begann seine Karriere bei Siemens und leitete unter anderem den Vertrieb der Siemens Nixdorf Informationssysteme in Hamburg. Von 1996 bis 2002 war er Vorstand der SAP SI AG und übernahm 2004 die Geschäftsleitung der Siemens Business Services Deutschland. Seit April 2009 ist er Vorstandsvorsitzender der TUDAG.

The author was born in Osnabrück in 1956 and studied in Clausthal and Munich. He started his career at Siemens and headed, among others, the sales of Siemens Nixdorf Information Systems in Hamburg. Later he was member of the bord of the SAP SI AG and then he was the Head of Siemens Business Services, Germany. Now he is chairman of the board of TUDAG since April 2009.

Die TUDAG Technische Universität Dresden AG ist als universitätsnahe Firmengruppe Teil der Gesamtstrategie der TU Dresden, um das enorme, täglich wachsende Wissen aus allen Fachbereichen effektiv der Wirtschaft zugänglich zu machen. Sie ist eine hundertprozentige Tochter der Gesellschaft von Freunden und Förderern der TU Dresden. Deren Mitglieder sind zu einem Großteil Unternehmen und Einzelpersönlichkeiten aus Wirtschaft und Gesellschaft, aber auch Alumni und zahlreiche Wissenschaftler der TU Dresden.

Bereits fünf Jahre nach der 1991 erfolgten Wiedergründung der Freundesgesellschaft wurde beschlossen, zur Vermarktung des Wissens der Universität in die im Kern erhaltene und nun wieder wachsende sächsische Industrie ein universitätsnahes Unternehmen zu gründen. So entstand die GWT-TUD GmbH als Gesellschaft für Wissens- und Technologietransfer.

Der Grundgedanke der von der Universitätsleitung mitinitiierten Unternehmensgründung bestand darin, den Wissenschaftlern eine Plattform für die Vermarktung innovationsträchtiger Ergebnisse aus Forschung und Entwicklung zu schaffen, ohne sie mit der Verantwortung eines Unternehmers zu belasten, und den Wirtschaftsunternehmen wiederum einen Ansprechpartner für die Zusammenarbeit mit der TU Dresden zu bieten. Der Gründungsgedanke hat sich bewährt. Die GWT entwickelte sich mit überdurchschnittlichem Umsatzwachstum zu einem weit über die Grenzen von Sachsen hinaus bekannten, zuverlässigen Partner der Industrie auf dem Gebiet des Know-how-Transfers aus Forschung und Entwicklung, Management und Beratung für neue Produkte und Technologien in nahezu allen Technologiefeldern.

Sie realisiert unternehmenskonkret Innovationen für die gesamte Wertschöpfungskette. Ihre Projektteams sind interdisziplinär zusammengesetzt. Dabei arbeiten je nach Aufgabenstellung nicht nur Wissenschaftler der TU Dresden zusammen, sondern es werden auch Experten anderer Hochschulen und Forschungseinrichtungen einbezogen. Der Anteil der mittelständischen Kunden überwiegt, mehr als 40 Prozent aller Vertragspartner kommen aus Sachsen. Das zeigt jedoch andererseits, dass die GWT schon lange nicht mehr nur regional agiert. Die Transferleistungen für Maschinenbauunternehmen und den Fahrzeugbau stellen mit wiederum über 40 Prozent den größten Umsatzanteil. Aber auch die Elektrotechnik- und Elektronikbranche stellt mit einem Viertel des Geschäftsvolumens einen beachtlichen Partner der GWT dar.

Science

Entwicklung und Herstellung einer Brücke aus textilbewehrtem Beton durch die Betonwerk Oschatz GmbH und die TU Dresden Auftragnehmer: GWT-TUD GmbH.
The development and production of a bridge made of textile-reinforced concrete by the Betonwerk Oschatz Gmbh and TU Dresden contractor: GWT-TUD GmbH.

Einschwenken der Fuß- und Radwegbrücke aus Textilbeton über die Rottach in Kempten.
Pivoting the pedestrian and cycling-lane bridge made of textile-reinforced concrete over the Rottach river in Kempten.

Entwicklungsauftrag der Automobilindustrie an die IAM.
The automotive industry's development request to IAM.

The TUDAG Technische Universität Dresden AG is an university-affiliated group of companies and part of the overall strategy of TU Dresden to make the day-to-day growing knowledge from all faculties accessible to the commercial market. It is a wholly owned subsidiary of the Association of Friends and Promoters of TU Dresden. Most members are companies and individuals from commerce and the community, but also former students and numerous academics of TU Dresden.

Five years after the reestablishment of the Association of Friends in 1991, it was already decided to establish a university-affiliated enterprise for the promotion of university knowledge into the Saxon industry, the core of which was retained and is now growing again. In this way the GWT-TUD GmbH originated as an association for the transfer of knowledge and technology.

The fundamental idea of the company foundation, which was initiated in cooperation whith the university management, was to create a platform for academics towards the promotion of hugely innovative achievements from research and development, without burdening them with entrepreneurial responsibilities, and in turn offering businesses a contact for collaboration with TU Dresden. The fundamental idea has proven itself. With an above-average growth in turnover, GWT has developed into a reliable industry partner – renowned well beyond the Saxon borders – in the area of know-how transfer from research and development, management and consulting for new products and technologies in almost all fields of technology. The GWT implements business-specific innovations for the entire value creation chain. Its project teams are put together to combine many disciplines. Therewith, according to task definition, not only do academics of the TU Dresden work together, but experts from other universities and research institutions are also involved. The proportion of medium-sized customers predominates, more than 40 per cent of all contractual partners are coming from Saxony. However, on the other hand it shows that GWT has no longer operated only regionally for a long time now. The transfer accomplishments of mechanical engineering enterprises and vehicle manufacturers, again with over 40 per cent, represent the largest share of turnover. However, the electro-technology and electronic industry with a quarter of the business volume also constitutes a formidable partner of GWT. The know-how transfer for the development of chemical commodities for the chemical industry, including the pharmaceutical industry and other industries, completes the network of close to 1,000 enterprises which for the most part constantly utilize their partnership with GWT. Therefore the distinction "Business 2006", which was awarded to GWT by the Bundesverband mittelständische Wirtschaft (a German association for the medium-sized sector) wasn't merely a welcomed prize, but rather documents the focus of economic activity on the medium-sized sector.

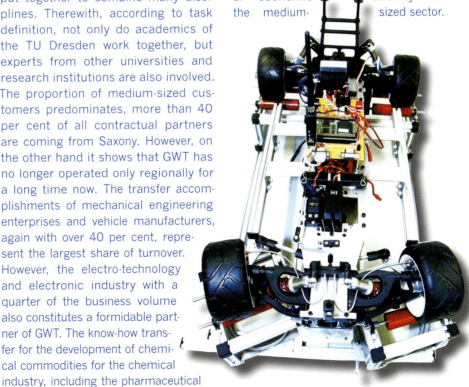

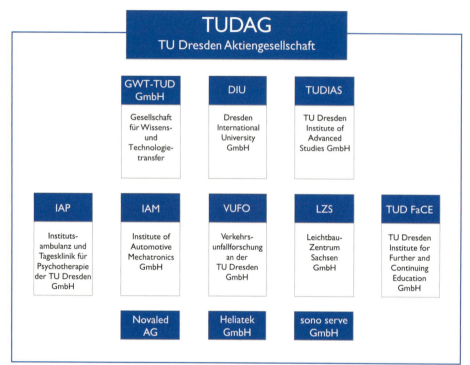

Zusammenarbeit zwischen der Wirtschaft und der TU Dresden: die Firmengruppe TUDAG.
Collaboration between the economy and TU Dresden: the TUDAG Group.

Know-how-Transfer zur Entwicklung chemischer Erzeugnisse für die Chemie, inklusive die Pharmaindustrie und die übrigen Branchen vervollständigt das Netzwerk der nahezu 1.000 Unternehmen, die zum großen Teil ständig die Partnerschaft mit der GWT nutzen. Von daher ist die Auszeichnung „Unternehmen 2006", die der GWT vom Bundesverband mittelständische Wirtschaft verliehen wurde, nicht nur ein willkommener Preis, sondern belegt den Fokus der Geschäftstätigkeit zum Mittelstand.

Im Jahre 2000 wurde vom Vorstand der Freundesgesellschaft und der Universitätsleitung die Entscheidung getroffen, die TUDAG zu gründen. Damit wurde eine neue Phase eingeleitet: die Chance der Entwicklung einer ganzen Firmengruppe unter dem Dach der TUDAG. Gleichzeitig konnte sich die TU-Freundesgesellschaft wieder auf ihren satzungsgemäßen Schwerpunkt konzentrieren, den gemeinnützigen Vereinszweck der Förderung von Forschung und Lehre der TU Dresden. Die Gründung der TUDAG wiederum dient auch dem Ziel, über Ausschüttungen den Vereinszweck immer umfangreicher erfüllen zu können. Aus der unternehmerischen Tätigkeit der Wissenschaftler mit Hilfe des GWT-Konstruktes hat sich in mehreren Fällen sehr bald gezeigt, dass die Gründung kleiner universitätsnaher Unternehmen mit einem definierten Produktportfolio weitere Wachstumschancen verspricht und die Zusammenarbeit mit der Wirtschaft fördert. So umfasst die TUDAG gegenwärtig neun Unternehmen und eine Reihe treuhänderischer Beteiligungen im Interesse der TU Dresden. Hervorzuheben ist auch, dass die kleinen Unternehmen wie das IAM Institute of Automotive Mechatronics GmbH, das Leichtbauzentrum Sachsen GmbH oder die VuFo Verkehrsunfallforschung an der TU Dresden GmbH schneller wachsen als die GWT. Dabei besteht aber auch für die GWT noch ein großes Potenzial für die Zukunft, da noch lange nicht alle Wissenschaftler und Institute der TU Dresden einerseits und die Industrie andererseits die Chancen des professionellen Know-how-Transfers nutzen.

Der Öffentlichkeitsarbeit kommt deshalb sowohl TU-intern als auch extern eine große Bedeutung zu, um die Vorteile für die kommerzielle Partnerschaft zwischen Wissenschaft und Wirtschaft erlebbar zu machen. Der Wissenschaftler kann flexibel unternehmerisch tätig werden, die Universität respektive sein Institut erhält über Infrastrukturnutzung, durch Investitionen in Maschinen und Anlagen erweiterte Spielräume für die grundständige Forschung und Lehre, Personaleinstellungen für junge Absolventen sind täglich steuerbar. Der Industrie wiederum wird in der kommerziellen Vertragspartnerschaft die Sicherheit der vereinbarten Leistungen auch hinsichtlich Qualität, Termin und eventueller Haftungsfragen gegeben.

Die TUDAG-Gruppe ist in ihrer Art einmalig in Deutschland. Ihre Gründer waren der Entwicklung voraus. Als Teil der Gesamtstrategie der Austauschprozesse zwischen TU Dresden und Unternehmen – von Stiftungslehrstühlen über strategische Partnerschaften mit Großunternehmen bis hin zu Existenzgründungen durch Absolventen und junge Wissenschaftler – erfüllt sie einen eindeutigen Auftrag: die zeitnahe, auf Innovationen in den Unternehmen ausgerichtete Partnerschaft. Voraussetzung hierfür ist die Fähigkeit der Partner, die häufigste Ausgangssituation „hier ist die Wissenskompetenz, da ist das Problem" zu einer problemgerechten Wertschöpfung bei unseren Kunden zu führen.

Science

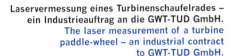

Laserschneidanlage.
Laser-cutting equipment.

Laservermessung eines Turbinenschaufelrades – ein Industrieauftrag an die GWT-TUD GmbH.
The laser measurement of a turbine paddle-wheel – an industrial contract to GWT-TUD GmbH.

In 2000, the decision to found TUDAG was taken by the board of directors of the Association of Friends and the university management. Therewith a new phase was set in motion: the opportunity for the development of a totally new group of companies under the new TUDAG umbrella. Simultaneously, the TU Association of Friends can again concentrate on its statutory focal points – the non-profit purpose of the association for the promotion of research and teaching at TU Dresden. The foundation of TUDAG in turn also serves the aim to fulfill the purpose of the association even more comprehensively by using profit distributions. From the entrepreneurial activities of academics with the help of the GWT construct, it was very quickly shown in many cases that the foundation of smaller university-related enterprises with a defined product portfolio promises further growth opportunities and promotes collaboration with the economy. In this way TUDAG currently comprises nine enterprises and an array of participations on a trust-basis in the interests of TU Dresden. It also has to be mentioned that the small enterprises – such as IAM Institute of Automotive Mechatronics GmbH, the Leichtbauzentrum Sachsen GmbH (light weight construction centre) or VuFo Verkehrsunfallforschung (traffic accident research) at the TU Dresden GmbH – are growing faster than GWT. However, there also exists great potential for GWT for the future as not all the academics and institutions at TU Dresden on the one hand and the industry on the other hand, have used the professional know-how transfer yet.

Therefore, public relations work is accorded great significance internally at TU Dresden as also externally, to tangibly experience the advantages of a commercial partnership between science and the economy. Academics can become flexible as regards entrepreneurial activity; the university or rather its institutions can, through the use of the infrastructure and through investments in machines and facilities, receive extended leeway for basic research and teaching; and staff appointments for young graduates are controllable on a daily basis. In the commercial partnership, the industry on the other hand is given the security of agreed performances also as regards quality, time limits and possible questions of liability.

The TUDAG Group is one-of-its-kind in Germany. Its founders were ahead of their times. As part of the overall strategy for the exchange processes between TU Dresden and organizations – from endowed chairs through strategic partnerships with large-scale enterprises to business start-ups by graduates and young academics – it fulfills an explicit task: the contemporary partnership aligned towards innovations in organizations. A prerequisite for this is the ability of partners to lead to an equitable creation of value for our customers in the most frequent initial situation "here is the scientific competence, there is the problem".

Company Profile

Fraunhofer-Institut für Werkstoff- und Strahltechnik IWS

Institutsleiter/Executive Director:
Prof. Dr.-Ing. habil. Eckhard Beyer

Gründungsjahr/Year of foundation: 1992

Mitarbeiter/Employees: 220

Umsatz/Turnover:
18 Millionen Euro/18 million euros

Geschäftstätigkeit/Business activity:
Fügen
Abtragen und Trennen
Randschichttechnik
Thermische Beschichtungstechnik
PVD-Vakuum-Schichttechnik
CVD-Atmosphärendruck-Schichttechnik
Joining
Removal and cutting
Surface treatment
Thermal coating
PVD · Vacuum coating technology
CVD · Atmospheric coating technology

Anschrift/Address:
Winterbergstraße 28
D-01277 Dresden
Telefon +49 (0) 351 2583-324
Telefax +49 (0) 351 2583-300
info@iws.fraunhofer.de
www.iws.fraunhofer.de

Beschichteter Solarwafer für die Photovoltaik.
Thermally coated solar wafer for photovoltaics.

Laserstrahlhärten von Turbinenschaufeln.
Laser beam hardening of turbine blades.

Fraunhofer IWS in Dresden.
Fraunhofer IWS in the city of Dresden.

Problemstellungen kundengerecht lösen
Customer-oriented problem solving

Das Fraunhofer IWS betreibt anwendungsorientierte Forschung auf den Gebieten der Laser- und Oberflächentechnik. Ausgeprägtes Werkstoff- und Nanotechnik-Know-how verbunden mit der Möglichkeit einer umfassenden Werkstoffcharakterisierung bilden die Grundlage der Forschungstätigkeiten.

Im Bereich der Lasertechnik konzentriert sich das IWS auf die werkstofforientierte Lasermaterialbearbeitung und die Entwicklung laserspezifischer Systemlösungen. Ziel ist es, innovative Technologien für Industrieunternehmen zu entwickeln und deren Einführung zu unterstützen.

In der Oberflächen- und Schichttechnik stehen Verschleißschutz, Oxidationsschutz und Funktionsschichten sowie das Abtragen, Strukturieren und Reparieren von Oberflächen im Mittelpunkt der Entwicklung. Dabei kommen verstärkt plasmabasierte Fertigungsverfahren zum Einsatz.

Durch die enge Zusammenarbeit mit Anlagen- und Systemanbietern bietet das IWS Problemlösungen aus einer Hand. Als Basis hierfür dient die Gesamtbetrachtung des Bearbeitungssystems, des Verfahrens sowie des Bauteilverhaltens. Die Ausstattung des Fraunhofer IWS mit modernster Anlagentechnik garantiert die effektive Bearbeitung von Aufgaben auf einem höchstmöglichen Niveau.

The Fraunhofer Institute for Material and Beam Technology (Fraunhofer IWS) carries out application-oriented research and development in the area of laser and surface technology. The basis of research activities is formed by highly developed materials and nanotechnology know-how linked with the possibility of comprehensive material characterization.

In the field of laser technology, IWS concentrates on materials-oriented laser materials processing and the development of laser-specific system solutions. The objective is to develop innovative technologies for industrial enterprises and to support the implementation thereof.

In the area of surface- and coating technology, the central focus of development lies in wear protection, oxidation protection and functional coatings as well as the removal, structuring and repair of surfaces. Thereby plasma-based finishing processes are increasingly applied.

Through close collaboration with facility and system providers, IWS offers one-stop solutions. The overall view of the processing system, the procedure as well as component performance serves as the basis thereof. The Fraunhofer IWS, equipped with the most modern systems technology, guarantees the effective handling of assignments at the highest possible level.

Company Profile

Anwendungsorientierte Forschung am Standort Dresden
Application-oriented research at the location of Dresden

**Fraunhofer-Institut
für Elektronenstrahl- und Plasmatechnik**

Geschäftsführer/Managing Directors:
Prof. Dr. Eberhard Schultheiß
Geschäftsf. Institutsleiter/Executive Director of Institute

Prof. Dr. Volker Kirchhoff
Kommis. Institutsleiter/Acting Director of Institute

Gründungsjahr/Year of foundation: 1992

Mitarbeiter/Employees:
102 Mitarbeiter
102 employees

Geschäftstätigkeit/Business activity:
Beschichtung von Flachsubstraten mit optischen Schichten und Schichtsystemen, Beschichtung von flexiblen Produkten, Beschichtung von Platten und metallischen Bändern, Oberflächenbearbeitung und -behandlung mit dem Elektronenstrahl, Beschichtung von Bauteilen und Werkzeugen, Beschichtung von optischen, elektronischen und magnetischen Komponenten
Coating of flat substrates with optical layers and layer systems, coating of flexible products, coating of sheets and metal strips, surface modification and treatment with electron beam, coating of machine parts and tools, coating of optic, electronic and magnetic components

Anschrift/Address:
Winterbergstraße 28
D-01277 Dresden
Telefon +49 (0) 351 2586-0
Telefax +49 (0) 351 2586-105
info@fep.fraunhofer.de
www.fep.fraunhofer.de

Das Fraunhofer-Institut für Elektronenstrahl- und Plasmatechnik FEP wurde nach der deutschen Wiedervereinigung aus Arbeitsgruppen des früheren Forschungsinstituts Manfred von Ardenne gegründet.
Ein wichtiges Arbeitsgebiet des Fraunhofer FEP ist die Dünnschichttechnologie. Dazu gehört die Beschichtung von Platten, Bändern und Bauteilen aus unterschiedlichen Materialien mit verschiedenen Schichten und Schichtsystemen. Viele Gegenstände des täglichen Lebens sind heute ohne angepasste Oberflächeneigenschaften nicht mehr denkbar, so zum Beispiel Verpackungsfolien oder Fassadenverkleidungen.
Ein weiteres wichtiges Arbeitsgebiet stellt darüber hinaus die Elektronenstrahltechnologie dar. Sie wird eingesetzt, um Metalle zu schweißen, zu verdampfen oder in der Randschicht zu modifizieren. So lassen sich Lacke härten oder die Eigenschaften von Kunststoff verbessern.
Die Forschungs- und Entwicklungstätigkeit des FEP zeichnet sich durch große Industrienähe und Kundenorientierung aus. Die wichtigsten Märkte sind dabei die Branchen Bau, Verkehr, Information, Maschinenbau, Pharmazie, Medizin und erneuerbare Energien. Unterstützt wird die Arbeit durch ein Geflecht von nationalen und internationalen Kooperationsbeziehungen.

Following the German reunion, the Fraunhofer Institute for Electron Beam and Plasma Technology FEP was established by working groups of the former Manfred von Ardenne R&D institute.
One main field of activity of the Fraunhofer FEP is the thin film technology. This includes coating of sheets, strips and components made of diverse materials with various layers or layer systems. Many items of our daily life like plastic web for packaging or facade cladding are not cogitable without adapted layer qualities.

The second main field of activity of the FEP is the electron beam technology. The electron beam is being used for the welding and evaporation of metals as well as for the modification in edge layers. Further applications are the curing of lacquers or the improvement of plastics properties.

Features of FEP's research and development are its customer-orientation and high relevance to industry. The important branches are the building industry, transport sector, information technology, engineering, pharmaceutics, medicine and renewable energy. A network of national and international co-operating partners is supporting this work.

**Das Fraunhofer FEP in Dresden und seine vertikale Inline Beschichtungsanlage ILA 900.
The Fraunhofer FEP in Dresden and the vertical inline sputter plant ILA 900.**

Anwendungsorientierte Forschung für die Unternehmen in der Region
Application-oriented research for organizations in the region

Prof. Dr. Eckhard Beyer
Der Autor wurde 1951 geboren. Nach Studienabschluss und Promotion als Dr. Ing. Physik an der TH Darmstadt arbeitete er zunächst zwölf Jahre am Fraunhofer ILT in Aachen. Seit 1997 ist Eckhard Beyer Leiter des Fraunhofer-Instituts für Werkstoff- und Strahltechnik (IWS) und fungiert ab 2009 als Sprecher des Fraunhofer-Institutszentrums in Dresden.
The author was born in 1951. After diploma and doctorate in physics at the Darmstadt University of Applied Sciences, he first worked at the Fraunhofer Institute for Laser Technology (ILT) in Aachen for twelve years. Since 1997 he has been the head of the Fraunhofer Institute for Material and Beam Technology (IWS) and will be acting as the spokesperson for the Fraunhofer Institution Centre in Dresden as from 2009.

Als 1992 mehrere Forschungs-Institute und Einrichtungen der neuen Bundesländer in die Fraunhofer-Gesellschaft aufgenommen wurden, bot sich in Dresden die einmalige Chance, Teile der besonders anwendungsorientierten Forschung fortzuführen und auszubauen. Inzwischen ist Dresden mit insgesamt sechs Instituten und fünf weiteren Einrichtungen zur heimlichen Fraunhofer-Hauptstadt Deutschlands geworden. Dank leistungsfähiger Infrastruktur und modernster Anlagentechnik erwirtschaften die Dresdner Institute heute einen jährlichen Umsatz von über 100 Millionen Euro und für die nächsten Jahre wird weiteres Wachstum angestrebt.

Die Fraunhofer-Institute in Dresden entwickeln Produkte und Verfahren bis zur industriellen Anwendung. Dabei werden in direktem Kontakt mit dem Auftraggeber individuelle Lösungen erstellt. Je nach Bedarf arbeiten mehrere Fraunhofer-Institute zusammen, um auch komplexe Systemlösungen zu realisieren. Die Ergebnisse stellen sie der Industrie als Patente, Lizenzen, Weiterbildungsangebote und vor allem in Form von Auftragsforschungsprojekten zur Verfügung. So profitieren die Unternehmen zahlreicher Branchen von der wissenschaftlich-technischen Kompetenz der Fraunhofer-Einrichtungen.

Das Fraunhofer-Institutszentrum Dresden auf der Winterbergstraße ist der zweitgrößte Fraunhofer-Standort in Deutschland und der größte in den neuen Bundesländern. Auf circa 26.000 Quadratmetern Technikums-, Labor- und Büroflächen wirken drei Fraunhofer-Institute und ein Teilinstitut. Gemeinsamkeit der Institute ist die Forschung und Entwicklung auf dem Gebiet der Material- und Energietechnologien.

So entwickelt beispielsweise das Fraunhofer IWS Plasmaquellen, die bei Atmosphärendruck arbeiten und sich damit besonders zur kostengünstigen Fertigung von Solarzellen eignen. Ein ebenso vielversprechender Ansatz zur Kostensenkung ist die In-Line-Fertigung siliziumbasierter Dünnschicht-Solarzellen in einem Vakuumprozess. Hier lassen die vom Fraunhofer FEP entwickelten PVD Technologien eine deutliche Reduzierung der Beschichtungskosten erwarten.

Research

Prozessoptimierung für die Solarzellenfertigung.
Process optimization for solar cell production.

FuE auf einen Blick: Die Broschüre „Fraunhofer in Dresden – Geballte Forschung" stellt die elf Dresdner Fraunhofer-Einrichtungen vor.
R&D at a glance: The brochure "Fraunhofer in Dresden – Geballte Forschung" ("Fraunhofer in Dresden – Research concentration") introduces the eleven Frauenhofer institutions.

In 1992, when several research institutions and establishments of the new federal states were absorbed into the Fraunhofer Gesellschaft (an organization for applied research), a golden opportunity presented itself in Dresden to continue and develop parts of the exceptional application-oriented research. In the meantime, Dresden has become the undercover Fraunhofer capital in Germany, with a total of six institutes and five other establishments. Thanks to efficient infrastructure and modern systems engineering, the Dresden institutions earn an annual turnover of more than 100 million euros, and further growth is aimed at for the next few years.

The Fraunhofer Institutes in Dresden develop products and processes right up to industrial application. In the process, individual solutions are constructed in direct contact with the client. Depending on requirements, several Fraunhofer institutions work together to also provide complex solutions. The results are made available to the industry in the form of patents, licenses, further education offers and primarily in the form of contract research projects. In this way, the organizations of numerous industries profit from the scientific-technical competence of the Fraunhofer institutions.

The Fraunhofer Institute Centre Dresden in Winterbergstraße is the second largest Fraunhofer location in Germany and the largest in the new federal states. Three Fraunhofer institutes and one member-institution operate technical, laboratory and office space of around 26,000 square metres. The institutions have research and development in the area of material and energy technology in common.

The Fraunhofer IWS, for instance, develops plasma sources which operate with atmospheric pressure and are thus particularly suited to the cost-effective production of solar cells. An equally promising approach to cost reduction is the in-line production of silicon-based thin film solar cells in a vacuum process. Here the PVD (physical vapor depositions coating) technologies developed by the Fraunhofer FEP (Fraunhofer Institute for Electron Beam and Plasma Technology) anticipate a notable reduction of surface coating costs. Already today, several in-line-capable vacuum technologies for the production of thin film solar cells are available and industrially implemented, for example pretreatment in vacuums and technologies for the deposition of insulation and barrier coatings, metallic contacts, transparent electrodes or anti-reflex and protective coatings.

As a contactless and well-automated tool, the laser also offers optimization potential in solar cell production.

Bereits heute sind einzelne in-Line-tauglichen Vakuumtechnologien zur Fertigung von Dünnschichtsolarzellen verfügbar und industriell eingeführt, beispielsweise die Vorbehandlung im Vakuum und Technologien zur Abscheidung von Isolations- und Barriereschichten, metallischen Kontakten, transparenten Elektroden oder Antireflex- und Schutzschichten.

Auch der Laser als berührungsloses und gut automatisierbares Werkzeug bietet Optimierungspotenzial in der Solarzellenfertigung. Technologieentwicklungen zum Schneiden und Kantenisolieren von mono- und multikristallinen Solarzellen, zur Herstellung von Kontaktbohrungen und Leiterbahnen, zur Strukturierung der Oberfläche, zur Verbesserung der Absorption der Sonneneinstrahlung sowie zum Verbinden der Solarzellen über Stringer zu Solarmodulen sind deshalb Entwicklungsschwerpunkte des Fraunhofer IWS. Und das von Wissenschaftlern des Instituts patentierte Laserstrahlhärten findet seit Jahren Anwendung im Bereich der klassischen Kraftwerkstechnik zur Verbesserung der Effizienz und Standfestigkeit von Laufschaufeln für Dampfturbinen.

Die Wissenschaftler des Fraunhofer IKTS haben zusammen mit Partnern aus der Industrie eine Technologie entwickelt, die Brennstoffzellen preisgünstig und langlebig macht. Sie eignen sich als mobile Stromgeneratoren für Campingfahrzeuge, Boote, Lkws oder Pkws, aber auch für stationäre Anwendungen zur Strom-, Wärme- und Kältegewinnung oder zur Verstromung von Biogas in der Landwirtschaft. Im Rahmen eines Forschungsprojektes zur regenerativen Energieerzeugung wird derzeit eine Anlage zur Bereitstellung von Strom und Wärme auf der Basis von nachwachsenden Rohstoffen konzipiert und gebaut.

Am Fraunhofer IFAM Dresden werden unter Anwendung und Weiterentwicklung pulvermetallurgischer Technologien Sinterwerkstoffe auf Basis von Metallen, Verbund- und Gradientenwerkstoffe für das thermische Management in der Elektronik sowie für thermoelektrische Werkstoffe, Reibwerkstoffe und Leichtmetalle entwickelt. Sehr geringe Dichte, sehr gute Schallabsorption, gutes thermisches Isoliervermögen und eine relativ hohe spezifische Oberfläche zeichnen die zellularen metallischen Werkstoffe des Fraunhofer IFAM aus.

Die drei großen Themenfelder „Verkehr Energie Umwelt" prägen auch das Profil des Fraunhofer IVI. Ob in großen nationalen Forschungsprojekten zu hybriden oder vollständig emissionsfreien Antriebstechnologien oder in den europäischen Projekten zur Entwicklung zuverlässiger Brennstoffzellenantriebe – stets ist sich

Entwicklung von Großformat-OLED-Leuchten im Fraunhofer IPMS.
The development of large-size OLED lamps at the Fraunhofer IPMS.

das Fraunhofer IVI seiner Verantwortung bei der Bewältigung aktueller und zukünftiger Aufgabenstellungen bewusst.

Ein weiteres Technologiefeld der Dresdner Fraunhofer-Institute ist die Mikroelektronik. Das Angebot des Fraunhofer IPMS richtet sich an Kunden, die die Funktionalität ihrer Produkte durch den Einsatz von organischen Leuchtdioden und Mikrosystemen mit innovativen Systemeigenschaften und immer kleineren Abmessungen erweitern wollen. Im Fokus stehen verschiedenste Applikationen, die in der Informationstechnologie, Medizintechnik, Umwelttechnologie, Sicherheitstechnik oder Automobilzulieferindustrie also in nahezu jedem Lebensbereich Einzug halten.

Research

Das Fraunhofer-Institutszentrum Dresden auf der Winterbergstraße bündelt Know-how auf dem Gebiet der Material- und Energietechnologien.
The Fraunhofer Institute Centre Dresden in Winterbergstraße bundles know-how in the area of material and energy technology.

Fraunhofer-Einrichtungen in Dresden

Fraunhofer-Center Nanoelektronische Technologien CNT
http://www.cnt.fraunhofer.de

Fraunhofer-Institut für Elektronenstrahl- und Plasmatechnik FEP
http://www.fep.fraunhofer.de

Fraunhofer-Institut für Keramische Technologien und Systeme IKTS
http://www.ikts.fraunhofer.de

Fraunhofer-Institut für Photonische Mikrosysteme IPMS
http://www.ipms.fraunhofer.de

Fraunhofer-Institut für Verkehrs- und Infrastruktursysteme IVI
http://www.ivi.fraunhofer.de

Fraunhofer-Institut für Werkstoff- und Strahltechnik IWS
http://www.iws.fraunhofer.de

Fraunhofer-Anwendungszentrum für Verarbeitungsmaschinen und Verpackungstechnik AVV
http://www.avv.fraunhofer.de

Fraunhofer IIS, Institutsteil Entwurfsautomatisierung EAS Dresden
http://www.eas.iis.fraunhofer.de

Fraunhofer IFAM, Institutsteil Dresden, Pulvermetallurgie und Verbundwerkstoffe
http://www.ifam-dd.fraunhofer.de

Fraunhofer-Institut für Werkzeugmaschinen und Umformtechnik IWU, Institutsteil Dresden
http://www.iwu.fraunhofer.de

Fraunhofer-Institut für Zerstörungsfreie Prüfverfahren IZFP, Institutsteil Dresden
http://www.izfp-d.fraunhofer.de

Technology development for the edge trimming and edge insulation of monocrystalline and multi-crystalline solar cells, for the production of contact drills and conducting paths, for the structuring of surfaces and for the improvement of solar radiation absorption as well as for the bonding of solar cells by stringers to solar panels, are therefore development focal points of the Fraunhofer IWS. And laser-beam hardening, which was patented by the scientists of the institute, has for many years found application in the field of classical power plant engineering for the improvement of efficiency and stability of rotor blades for steam turbines.

The scientists of the Fraunhofer IKTS Fraunhofer Institute for Ceramic Technologies and Systems), together with industry partners, have developed a technology that makes fuel cells cheaper and durable. They are suitable as mobile power generators for camping vehicles, boats, freight vehicles or motor cars, but also in stationary applications for the recovery of energy, heat and coolness or for the conversion of biogas into electricity in agriculture. A facility for the provision of electricity and heat on the basis of renewable raw materials is being designed and built within the framework of a research project for regenerative energy production.

At the Fraunhofer IFAM Dresden (Fraunhofer Institute for Manufacturing and Advanced Materials), sinter materials, which are based on metals, composite and gradient materials for thermal management in electronics as well as for thermoelectric materials, friction materials and light metals are being developed according to the application and advancement of powder metallurgical technologies. The cellular metallic materials of the Fraunhofer IFAM are characterized by very low density, excellent acoustic absorption, good thermal insulation ability and a relatively high specific surface area.

The three large topics "traffic – energy – environment" also characterize the profile of the Fraunhofer IVI (Fraunhofer Institute for Transportation and Infrastructure Systems). Whether in large national research projects for hybrid or complete emission-free driving technology or in European projects for the development of reliable fuel cell engines – the Fraunhofer IVI is continually aware of its responsibility towards the accomplishment of current and future tasks.

A further technology field of the Dresden Fraunhofer Institutes is microelectronics. The Fraunhofer IPMS (Fraunhofer Institute for Photonic Microsystems) range is directed at clients who wish to enhance the functionality of their products through the application of organic light-emitting diodes and microsystems with innovative system properties and ever-decreasing dimensions.

Forschung

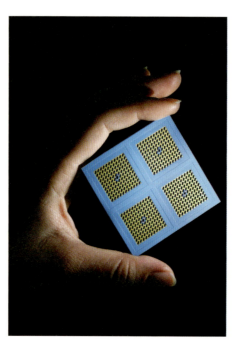

Die integrierte keramische Brennstoffzelle: klein, handlich und kostengünstig.
Integrated ceramic fuel cells: small, handy and cheap.

Im Fraunhofer CNT forschen Wissenschaftler auf 800 Quadratmetern Reinraumfläche Tür an Tür zur Halbleiterfertigung von Quimonda und AMD.
At the Fraunhofer CNT scientists do research on a cleanroom area of 800 square metres, door-to-door with semiconductor producers Quimonda and AMD.

Das Fraunhofer CNT, das als Public Private Partnership zwischen der Fraunhofer-Gesellschaft, AMD Inc. und der Qimonda AG gegründet wurde, forscht in unmittelbarer Nachbarschaft zu den Halbleiterherstellern an Weiterentwicklungen in den Bereichen Neue Materialien, innovative Prozessierungstechnologien sowie Metrologie und Analytik auf atomarer Ebene. Modernste Geräte ermöglichen die Waferprozessierung mit neuen und etablierten Methoden sowie das Testen innovativer Materialkombinationen.

Der rechnergestützte Entwurf elektronischer Schaltungen ist schon seit circa 50 Jahren Gegenstand wissenschaftlicher Arbeiten in Dresden. Heute werden im Institutsteil EAS des Fraunhofer IIS international anerkannte Verfahren für den rechnergestützten Entwurf von elektronischen und zunehmend von heterogenen Systemen entwickelt. Die erarbeiteten Modelle, Methoden und Werkzeuge dienen der Umsetzung von Produktspezifikationen in Schaltkreise, elektronische Geräte beziehungsweise heterogene Systeme.

Profilbestimmend für das Fraunhofer IZFP Dresden ist die Entwicklung von Systemen zur Zustandsüberwachung für Kunden aus der Luft- und Raumfahrt, Umwelttechnik und der chemischen Industrie. In der Industrie werden die auf akustischen und optischen Techniken basierenden Arbeitsergebnisse überall dort eingesetzt, wo sicherheitstechnische Aussagen und Qualitätsnachweise gefordert sind.

Die Entwicklung intelligenter Produktionsanlagen, verbunden mit der Optimierung der diesbezüglichen Fertigungsprozesse, ist Forschungsschwerpunkt des Fraunhofer IWU. Am Standort Dresden werden hochintegrierte intelligente Systeme für den Maschinen- und Fahrzeugbau auf Basis von „smart materials" entwickelt. Im Mittelpunkt stehen aktive Komponenten und Multifunktionswerkstoffe sowie die akustische Analyse für den Maschinenbau und die Fahrzeugtechnik.

Geht es um die gesamtheitliche Betrachtung der in Verpackungsprozessen stattfindenden komplexen Wechselwirkungen zwischen Füllgut, Packmittel und Maschine, ist das Fraunhofer AVV ein leistungsfähiger und qualifizierter Dienstleister für industrielle Forschungs- und Entwicklungsarbeiten.

Die elf Fraunhofer-Einrichtungen beschäftigen zusammen mehr als 1.100 Mitarbeiter. Der alljährlich für herausragende in die industrielle Nutzung überführte wissenschaftliche Leistungen vergebene Preis der Fraunhofer-Gesellschaft ging seit 1992 bereits acht Mal an Dresdner Institute, ein Beweis für die Innovationskraft der Dresdner Fraunhofer-Forscher.

Research 55

Nachwuchsforum am Fraunhofer IWS
im Rahmen der Nanofair 2008 Dresden.
A junior forum at the Fraunhofer IWS
within the scope of Nanofair 2008 Dresden.

Elektronisches Fahrgeldmanagement:
das ALLFA-Ticket im Probebetrieb.
Electronic fare management:
the ALLFA ticket on trial operation.

The focal point lies in the most diverse applications that find their way into information technology, medical engineering, environmental technology, safety engineering or the automotive supply industry, thus in almost all areas of life.

The Fraunhofer CNT (Fraunhofer Centre for Nanoelectronic Technologies), which was founded as a public-private partnership between the Fraunhofer Gesellschaft, AMD Inc. (Advanced Micro Devices Incorporated) and the Quimonda AG, in the immediate proximity of the semiconductor producers, does research on further development in the areas: new materials, innovative processing technology as well as metrology and chemical analysis at atomic level. The most modern equipment allows for wafer processing with new and established methods as well as the testing of innovative material combinations.

The computer-based design of electronic connectors has already been the object of scientific work in Dresden for almost 50 years. Today, the EAS section (design automation) of the Fraunhofer IIS (Fraunhofer Institute for Integrated Circuits) develops internationally recognized processes for computer-based design of electronic and increasingly of heterogeneous systems.

A profile-determining attribute of the Fraunhofer IZFP (Fraunhofer Institute for Non-Destructive Testing) is the development of systems for equipment condition monitoring for clients in the aerospace, environmental engineering and chemical industries. In industry, the results based on acoustic and optical technologies are deployed in all instances where safety-related evidence and quality verification is required.

The development of intelligent production facilities, combined with the optimization of production processes relating to this, constitutes the research focus of the Fraunhofer IWU (Fraunhofer Institute for Machine Tools and Forming Technology). At the Dresden location, highly integrated intelligent systems for machine and vehicle construction are developed on the basis of "smart materials". The centre stage is taken by active components and multifunctional materials as well as the acoustic analysis for machine construction and vehicle technology.

When the complex interaction between filling, packaging and machinery taking place in the packaging processes is considered in its entirety, the Fraunhofer AVV (Fraunhofer Application Center for Processing Machinery and Packaging Technology) is an effective and qualified service provider for industrial research and development work.

The eleven Fraunhofer institutions together employ more than 1,100 people. The annual prize awarded by the Fraunhofer Gesellschaft for the conversion of outstanding scientific performance into industrial use, has been awarded to Dresden institutes eight times already since 1992, a demonstration of the innovative energy of the Dresden Fraunhofer researchers.

Company Profile

Max-Planck-Institut für Chemische Physik fester Stoffe

Geschäftsführender Direktor/ Managing Director:
Prof. Juri Grin

Direktoren am Institut/ Collegium of directors:
Prof. Juri Grin
(Chemische Metallkunde/Chemical Metal Science)
Prof. Dr. Rüdiger Kniep
(Anorganische Chemie/Inorganic Chemistry)
Prof. Dr. Frank Steglich
(Festkörperphysik/Solid State Physics)

Gründungsjahr/Year of foundation:
1995

Arbeitsaufnahme/Business start-up:
1996

Mitarbeiter/Employees:
180

Anschrift/Address:
Nöthnitzer Straße 40
D-01187 Dresden
Telefon +49 (0) 351 4646-3602
Telefax +49 (0) 351 4646-10
www.cpfs.mpg.de

Max-Planck-Institut erforscht metallreiche Verbindungen
The Max Planck Institute investigates compounds rich in metal

Das Max-Planck-Institut für Chemische Physik fester Stoffe widmet sich der experimentellen und theoretischen Erforschung metallreicher Verbindungen mit neuartigen chemischen und physikalischen Eigenschaften. Voraussetzung zur Lösung der Fragestellungen ist die enge Zusammenarbeit zwischen den drei Forschungsbereichen Festkörperphysik, Anorganische Chemie und Chemische Metallkunde sowie die intensive Wechselwirkung mit und zwischen den Kompetenz- und Nachwuchsgruppen. Die flexible und multidisziplinäre Struktur des Instituts ermöglicht es, schnell und effizient Projektgruppen zu aktuellen Themen zu bilden, in denen Wissenschaftler gruppenübergreifend ihr jeweiliges Know-how einbringen. Die Hauptforschungsgebiete des Instituts sind derzeit orientiert auf:
- Quantenkritische Phänomene
- Chemische Bindung in intermetallischen Verbindungen
- Supraleitung und Magnetismus
- Struktur-Eigenschaftsbeziehungen in metallreichen Verbindungen
- Phasengleichgewichte, Phasenumwandlungen
- Entwicklung neuer Synthesemethoden
- Neue Materialklassen
- Thermoelektrika
- Biomineralisation

Das Institut ist mit seinen Forschungsschwerpunkten aktiv in nationale und internationale Netzwerke eingebunden.

The Max Planck Institute for Chemical Physics of Solids dedicates itself to the experimental and theoretical investigation of compounds rich in metal with novel chemical and physical characteristics. A precondition for the resolution of questions is the close collaboration between the three research fields of Solid States Physics, Inorganic Chemistry and Chemical Metal Science as well as the intensive interaction with and between the competence and junior groups. The flexible and multi disciplinary structure of the institute allows for the fast and efficient accumulation of current topics into project groups, into which scientists can introduce their respective know-how across the groups. The primary research fields of the institute are currently oriented towards:
- Quantum critical phenomena
- Chemical bonding in intermetallic compounds
- Superconductivity and magnetism
- Structure relationships in compounds rich in metal
- Phase equilibrium, phase transformation
- Development of new synthesis techniques
- New material classes
- Thermoelectrica
- Biomineralization

The institute is actively integrated in national and international networks with its research focal points.

Max-Planck-Institut für Physik komplexer Systeme
Max Planck Institute for the Physics of Complex Systems

Das Institut vertritt die Physik komplexer Systeme von der klassischen Physik bis zur Quantenphysik in drei Schwerpunkten, geformt durch die Forschung der drei permanenten Abteilungen. In der Quantenphysik forscht die *Abteilung Kondensierte Materie* in der Festkörperphysik. Mit Hilfe semiklassischer Methoden studiert die *Abteilung Endliche Systeme* nichtlineare Phänomene in der Dynamik von Atomen, Molekülen und Clustern. In der klassischen Physik widmet sich die *Abteilung Biologische Physik* mit Mitteln der statistischen Physik biologischen Themen. Eine permanente sowie drei temporäre Arbeitsgruppen, drei Nachwuchsgruppen und eine Emmy-Noether-Gruppe verstärken und verzahnen die Forschung der einzelnen Gruppen auf solchen Gebieten wie nichtlineare Zeitreihenanalyse, mesoskopische Systeme, intensive Laserfelder in Medien, stochastische Prozesse in der Biophysik, Physik des Geruchssinns, Motorsysteme, Dynamik biologischer Netzwerke sowie nichtlineare und relativistische Optik. Ein großes Gästeprogramm erlaubt etwa 70 Gastwissenschaftlern aus mehr als 20 Nationen, am Institut zu forschen sowie 15–20 Workshops im Jahr durchzuführen. Letztere bieten neuen Forschungsrichtungen ein Forum und haben das Ziel, den wissenschaftlichen Nachwuchs rasch mit sich neu entwickelnden Gebieten vertraut zu machen.

The Max Planck Institute represents the physics of complex systems from classical physics right up to quantum physics in three focal points formed by research in three permanent departments. In quantum physics, the *Department of Condensed Matter Physics* does research in solid-state physics. With the assistance of semi-classical methods the *Department of Finite Systems* studies non-linear phenomena in atomic, molecular and cluster dynamics. In classical physics, the *Biological Physics Department* addresses biological topics with the use of statistical physics. A permanent as well as three non-tenured research groups, three junior research groups and one Emmy-Noether group strengthen and interconnect the research of individual groups in areas such as non-linear time-series analysis, mesoscopic systems, intense laser fields in media, stochastic processes in biophysics, biological physics of olfaction, motor systems, dynamics of biological networks, as well as non-linear and relativistic optics. A large guest programme allows for approximately 70 visiting scientists from more than 20 nations to do research at the institute, at a time as well as to conduct 15 to 20 workshops per year. The latter offer a forum for new research fields and have the objective of rapidly acquainting young scientists with the new developing areas.

Max-Planck-Institut für Physik komplexer Systeme

Direktorium/Board of Directors:
Dr. Roderich Moessner
Prof. Dr. Frank Jülicher
Prof. Dr. Jan-Michael Rost

Geschäftsführender Direktor/ Managing Director:
Prof. Dr. Jan-Michael Rost

Gründungsjahr/Year of foundation:
1992

Mitarbeiter/Employees:
185

Anschrift/Address:
Nöthnitzer Straße 38
D-01187 Dresden
Telefon +49 (0) 351 871-0
Telefax +49 (0) 351 871-1999
info@pks.mpg.de
www.pks.mpg.de

BIOPOLIS Dresden –
Eine Vision wird Wirklichkeit
BIOPOLIS Dresden –
A vision becomes reality

Prof. Dr. Kai Simons

Kai Simons promovierte 1965 an der Universität in Helsinki und war dort Professor für Biochemie. 1975 wurde er Gruppenleiter am Europäischen Molekular Biologie Laboratorium in Heidelberg und leitete bis 1998 das Zell-Biologie-Programm. Er ist Gründungsdirektor des Max-Planck-Insitutes für Molekulare Zellbiologie und Genetik in Dresden. Seit 2002 ist er Vorstandsvorsitzender des BioDresden eV.

Kai Simons obtained his doctorate at the university in Helsinki in 1965 and was professor for biochemistry there. In 1975 he became the group leader at the European Molecular Biology Laboratory in Heidelberg and headed the Cell Biology Programme until 1998. He is the founding director of the Max Planck Institute of Molecular Cell Biology and Genetics in Dresden. He has been the chairperson of the board of BioDresden eV since 2002.

Dresden ist nicht nur das „Sächsische Silicon Valley" mit einer Spitzenstellung im Bereich Mikroelektronik. Die Region Dresden arbeitet mit einem enormen Kraftaufwand auch an dem ehrgeizigen Projekt, die Biotechnologie zu einem zweiten Standbein zu machen und damit die Vision *BIOPOLIS Dresden* zu verwirklichen.

Der Motor für dieses Projekt war die Gründung des Max-Planck-Institutes für Molekulare Zellbiologie und Genetik (MPI-CBG). Der Aufbau wurde durch 100 Millionen Euro der sächsischen Staatsregierung gefördert und ist mit einem 25-Millionen-Euro-„InnoRegio" Forschungsprojekt des Bundesministeriums für Bildung und Forschung bewilligt. Dies führte zur Schaffung eines neuen Zentrums – des Bioinnovationszentrum in Johannstadt, in dem biologische Grundlagenforschung und neu gegründete Biotechnologiefirmen unter einem Dach arbeiten. Heute bilden die außeruniversitären Forschungsinstitute, einschließlich des MPI-CBG, des Max-Planck-Instituts für Physik komplexer Systeme und des Max Bergmann Zentrums für Biomaterialien sowie des Biotechnologischen Zentrums (Biotec) und des Medizinisch Theoretischen Zentrums der TU Dresden, ein dichtes Netzwerk, sowohl in der Lehre als auch in der Forschung. Mehr als 600 Wissenschaftler arbeiten in diesem biotechnologischen Ballungsgebiet. Dresden wurde so rasch durch seine Forschung in den „Life Sciences" überall in der Welt bekannt.

Die Attraktivität dieses Forschungsumfeldes wird durch den Erfolg des Doktoranden-Programms unterstrichen, welches Studenten aus über 30 Ländern ausbildet. Es beherbergt circa 230 Doktoranden und ist eines der größten des Landes. Ein Grund für den Erfolg ist der fächerübergreifende Ansatz in Zellbiologie, Genetik, Biophysik, Neurobiologie, Stammzellenbiologie und Bioingenieurwesen.

Diese Ballung der Forschung ist verstärkt worden durch die Exzellenzinitiative des BMBF – die Etablierung des „Exzellenz Clusters für Regenerative Therapien-CRTD". Die Initiative wird aktuell im BioInnovationsZentrum, im Biotec der Technischen Universität Dresden durchgeführt, und der Einzug in den neu zu errichtenden Teil des Gebäudes wird 2010 erwartet.

Dieser Aufbau von Forschungskompetenzen ist begleitet worden durch eine Welle von Ausgründungen. Dresden hat heute 25 Biotech-Firmen, in der 1.547 Leute angestellt sind. Eine Reihe der Biotech-Firmen ist im BioInnovationsZentrum, in dem auch Spitzenwissenschaftler der Biotechnologie der Technischen Universität angesiedelt sind.

Biotechnology

Altes und neues Dresden: Frontansicht des geplanten Forschungszentrum für „Regenerative Therapien" und die Frauenkirche.
The old and new Dresden: frontal view of the planned research centre for "Regenerative Therapies" and the Frauenkirche.

Dresden is not only the "Saxon Silicon Valley" with a leading position in the field of microelectronics. The Dresden region puts tremendous effort also in the ambitious project which would make biotechnology a second supporting pillar and therewith achieve the vision of BIOPOLIS Dresden.

The driving force behind this project was the foundation of the Max Planck Institute of Molecular Cell Biology and Genetics (MPI-CBG). The development was aided by 100 million euros from the Saxon state government and the allotment of a 25-million-euro "InnoRegio" research project by the Federal Ministry of Education and Research (BMBF). This lead to the creation of a new centre – the BioInnovationCenter in Johannstadt, where biological basic research and newly founded biotechnology organizations work together under one roof. Today a dense network has been generated by non-university research institutions, including the MPI-CBG, the Max Planck Institute for the Physics of Complex Systems and the Max Bergmann Centre for Biomaterials as well as the Biotechnology Centre (Biotec) and the Medical Theoretical Centre of the Dresden University of Technology, in teaching as well as in research. More than 600 scientists work in this biotechnology concentration area. Dresden has rapidly become known everywhere in the world due to its research in the "life sciences".

The attractiveness of this research field is emphasized by the success of the postgraduate programme, which educates students from more than 30 countries. It accommodates around 230 postgraduates and is one of the largest in the country. One reason for the success is the interdisciplinary approach in cell biology, genetics, biophysics, neurobiology, stem cell biology and bioengineering.

This concentration of research has been strengthened by the excellence initiative of the BMBF – the establishment of of the "Excellence Clusters for Regenerative Therapy-CRTD". The initiative is currently being carried out in the BioInnovationCenter at Biotec at the Dresden University of Technology. Occupation of the section to be newly-erected is expected in 2010.

Das sind zum Beispiel die Firmen *Cenix BioScience GmbH*, *Jado Technologies GmbH*, *Ambition GmbH*, *InnoTERE GmbH*, *Gene Bridges GmbH*, *Scionics Computer Innovation GmbH*, *Transinsight GmbH*, *NAMOS GmbH*, *HPC BioInno Tec GmbH* und *Biote(a)ch*. Das sind zumeist kleine Firmen, die unter anderem in der pharmazeutischen Diagnostik, Bioinformatik oder in Servicebereichen arbeiten. Auch größere Pharmaunternehmen agieren in Dresden. *GlaxoSmithKline Biologicals* eröffnete 2007 einen Ergänzungsbau zur Impfstoffherstellung, der im Februar 2008 voll in Betrieb genommen wurde. Auch in Hellerau, einem anderen Stadtteil von Dresden, ist ein neues Biotechnologie Zentrum mit sechs Firmen, wie zum Beispiel den Firmen *Biotype AG*, *Labordiagnostik GmbH Leipzig* und *Qualitype AG* gegründet worden.

Dresden investiert jedoch auch in ein weiteres Zukunftsgebiet, die Nanotechnologie, deren Forschungsanstrengungen aktuell stark unterstützt werden.

Unser gegenwärtiges Technologiefundament beginnt zu wanken. Die fossilen Ressourcen und metallischen Rohstoffe, welche wir benutzen, um unseren Wohlstand sicherzustellen, unterliegen einem ansteigenden Verbrauch bei begrenztem Vorrat. Eine zentrale Aufgabe ist es deshalb, neue Technologien zu entwickeln, die nachhaltig sind und auf effizienteren Prinzipien beruhen. Die Miniaturisierung ist der Schlüssel dazu. Vom mikrotechnologischen Zeitalter müssen wir in die Nanotechnologie überwechseln – unsere mikrotechnologischen Instrumente müssen tausendfach kleiner werden. Für diese technologische Revolution sind wir darauf angewiesen, von der Natur zu lernen. Die biologische Forschung wird daher eine entscheidende Rolle spielen. Alle Organismen auf diesem Planeten enthalten kleine Maschinen, Nanomaschinen. Sie bestehen aus verschiedenen Proteinen und sind äußerst leistungsfähig. Zellen enthalten zum Beispiel „Müllverarbeitungsanlagen" mit hervorragenden Recyclingkapazitäten und winzige Motoren,

die für die Transport- und Kommunikationssysteme verantwortlich sind. Biologische Systeme arbeiten nach nanotechnologischen Prinzipien. Die Biologie ist Nanotechnologie und die Zukunftstechnologie wird die Bionanotechnologie sein.

Was heute in der Öffentlichkeit diskutiert wird, die rote und die grüne Biotechnologie, die Gentechnik und die Stammzellenforschung, ist nur ein kleiner Teil davon, was Biotechnologie in der Zukunft ausmachen wird. Riesige Anstrengungen werden notwendig sein, um diese Neuentwicklungen zu ermöglichen.

Die Ingenieure der Zukunft werden ihre Inspirationen von der Biologie erhalten. Somit müssen neue Nahtstellen zwischen Biologie und Engineering entwickelt werden. Die TU Dresden hat dazu das Molecular Bioengineering Programm ZIK B-CUBE gestartet. Die neue Initiative ist vom Bundesministerium für Bildung und Forschung (BMBF) finanziert und soll den weiteren Aufbau von *BIOPOLIS Dresden* in diesem neuen Forschungsgebiet vorantreiben.

Biotechnology

Biologen oder Ingenieure?
Junge Naturwissenschaftler entwickeln mit ihren Forschungsarbeiten aus der Biotechnologie heraus die künftige Nanotechnologie.
**Biologists or engineers?
With their research work, young scientists develop the future nanotechnology from biotechnology.**

This concentration of research competencies has been accompanied by a wave of new company foundations. Today Dresden has 25 biotech companies, which employ 1,547 people. A number of biotech companies are in the BioInnovationCenter, in which leading scientists of biotechnology at the University of Technology are also resident.
They are for example the companies *Cenix BioScience GmbH, Jado Technologies GmbH, Ambition GmbH, InnoTERE GmbH, Gene Bridges GmbH, Scionics Computer Innovation GmbH, Transinsight GmbH, NAMOS GmbH, HPC BioInno Tec GmbH* and *Biote(a)ch*. They are mainly small companies that amongst other things work in pharmaceutical diagnostics, bioinformatics or in the service areas in Dresden. Larger pharmaceutical companies also operate in Dresden. *GlaxoSmithKline Biologicals* opened an additional building for the production of vaccines in 2007, which was taken into full operation in February 2008. In Hellerau, another quarter in Dresden, a new biotechnology centre was also founded with six companies such as *Biotype AG, Labordiagnostik GmbH Leipzig* and *Qualitype AG*.

Dresden however also invests in another future area – nanotechnology, the research activities of which are currently strongly supported.

Our existing technology foundation is starting to shake. The fossil resources and metallic raw materials we use to ensure our prosperity, are subject to an increased consumption with limited supply. It is therefore a key task to develop technologies that are sustainable and are based on more efficient principles. Miniaturization is the key thereto. We must switch from the micro-technological age into nanotechnology – our micro-technological instruments have to become a thousand times smaller. For this technological revolution, we have to learn from nature. Biological research will therefore play a decisive role. All organisms on this planet contain small machines, nanomachines. They consist of different proteins and are extremely capable. Cells, for instance, contain "waste processing facilities" with outstanding recycling capacities and tiny motors that are responsible for transport and communication systems. Biological systems work according to nanotechnological principles. Biology is nanotechnology and the technology of the future will be bio-nanotechnology.

What is publically debated today – red and green biotechnology, gene technology and stem cell research – is only a small part of what will in future constitute biotechnology. Tremendous efforts will be necessary to make these new developments possible.

The engineers of the future will obtain their inspiration from biology. Consequently, new interfaces between biology and engineering should be developed.

Weiterhin wurde kürzlich das Spitzencluster „Cool Silicon" gegründet, dessen Zentrum Dresden bildet. Das BMBF und industrielle Quellen finanzieren das Vorhaben mit 200 Millionen Euro. Ziel von „Cool Silicon" ist es, die technologischen Grundlagen für eine massive Steigerung der Energieeffizienz im Bereich der Informations- und Kommunikationstechnologie zu schaffen. In der Zukunft müssen die Initiativen B-CUBE und Cool Silicon Technologien entwickeln und geschäftlich verwerten, um Dresden in ein globales Hochtechnologie-Zentrum zu verwandeln, welches von einer Forschung von Weltrang angeführt wird.

BIOPOLIS Dresden ist ein Kind des 21. Jahrhunderts. Weniger als zehn Jahre nach seiner Gründung ist diese Wissenschaftsschmiede ein Name im globalen Dorf der Zukunftstechnologien geworden. Wir können nur hoffen, dass die Finanzkrise von 2008 ein Zeichen für die Welt ist, in eine umweltverträgliche Zukunft zu investieren anstatt in eine Inventur des virtuellen Geldes, welches sich nun in Rauch aufgelöst hat.

Biotechnology

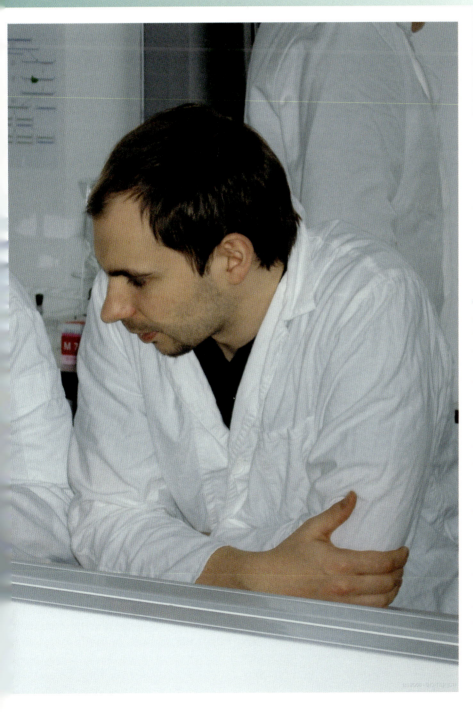

For this purpose, the Dresden University of Technology has started the molecular bioengineering programme ZIK B-CUBE. The new initiative is being financed by the Federal Ministry of Education and Research (BMBF) and should advance the further development of *BIOPOLIS Dresden* in this new research area.

Furthermore, the leading-edge cluster "Cool Silicon" was founded recently, of which Dresden forms the focal point. The BMBF and industrial sources are funding the project with 200 million euros. The objective of "Cool Silicon" is to create technological foundations for a massive boost in energy efficiency in the area of information and communications technology. In future, the initiatives B-CUBE and Cool Silicon will have to develop and commercialize technologies to transform Dresden into a global high-technology centre where world-class research is offered.

BIOPOLIS Dresden is a child of the 21st century. Less than ten years after its foundation, this hotbed of science has become a name in the global city of future technologies. We can only hope that the financial crisis of 2008 is a signal to the world to invest in an ecologically compatible future instead of in the inventory of virtual currency, which has now vanished into thin air.

Company Profile

Glatt Systemtechnik GmbH, Dresden (GST)

Geschäftsführer/Managers:
Reinhard Nowak,
Ralf Kretzschmar

Gründungsjahr/Year of foundation:
1991

Mitarbeiter/Employees:
190

Geschäftstätigkeit/Business activity:
- Komplettausrüster für die Branchen Pharmaherstellung, Nahrungs- und Futtermittelproduktion, Feinchemie, Life Science mit den Schwerpunkten Nassgranulationstechnik, komplexe Handlingsysteme für feste, fließfähige Produkte, Total-Containment-Systeme, Siebtechnik, Laboranlagen.
- Entwicklung innovativer Werkstoffe auf der Basis metallischer Hohlkugeln
- „Technikum" für Forschung und Entwicklung für oben genannte Branchen
- Full-service supplier to the pharmaceuticals manufacturing, foodstuffs, animal feed, fine chemicals, life sciences industries, concentrating on wet granulation technology, complex handling systems for firm, fluid products, total-containment systems, sieve technology and laboratory equipment.
- Development of innovative materials on the basis of metallic hollow spheres.
- "Technikum" for research and development for the above-mentioned sectors

Anschrift/Address:
Grunaer Weg 26
D-01277 Dresden
Telefon +49 (0) 351 2584-325
Telefax +49 (0) 351 2584-328
info.dd@glatt.com
www.glatt.com

Postanschrift/Postal address:
PF/PO Box 20 09 32
D-01194 Dresden

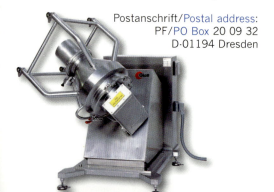

Modernste Pharmatechnik für Kunden in aller Welt
The latest pharmaceutical technology for customers all over the world

Die Glatt Systemtechnik GmbH entstand 1991 aus einem Betriebsteil der Hochvakuumtechnik Dresden (HVD) mit langjähriger Erfahrung im hochspezialisierten Präzisions- und Verfahrensanlagenbau. Heute ist das Unternehmen ein wichtiger Produktionsstandort der Glatt-Gruppe mit Hauptsitz im badischen Binzen. In Dresden werden moderne Maschinen, Anlagen und Ausrüstungen der Erzeugnisreihen Produkt-Handling, Total-Containment, Nass- und Trockenmischer, Siebe und Pelletierer für die Branchen Pharma, Food, Feed, Fine Chemicals und Life Science hergestellt.

Mit 190 hochmotivierten Mitarbeitern, davon circa 35 in Forschung und Entwicklung, liegt der Schwerpunkt bei der Entwicklung und Fertigung komplexer Applikationen, die in die ganze Welt geliefert werden. Ein modern ausgerüstetes „Technikum" steht dem Kunden für die Entwicklung und Optimierung neuer Produkte und Verfahren zur Verfügung. Seit 1991 wurden für namhafte Firmen, wie zum Beispiel Bayer-Schering, Sanofi-Aventis, AstraZeneca, Novartis, Merck und Teva, eine Reihe von Großprojekten weltweit realisiert. In enger Kooperation mit Partnern aus der Forschung und Wirtschaft ist Glatt an der Entwicklung und Produktion von neuartigen und leichten Werkstoffen für verschiedene Industrien (zum Beispiel Automobil- und Anlagenbau) beteiligt.

Glatt Systemtechnik GmbH was formed in 1991 from a part of Hochvakuumtechnik Dresden (HVD), which had many years of experience in the construction of high-precision and process technology plants. Today the company is an important manufacturing location of the Glatt Group, headquartered in the south of Germany, in Binzen. Glatt Systemtechnik GmbH makes modern machinery, plants and equipment for product series like product handling, total containment, wet and dry mixers, sieves and spheronizers for the pharmaceutical, food, feed, fine chemical and life science industries.

With 190 highly motivated employees, 35 are involved in research and development, the main emphasis of the company's activities is on the development and production of complex solutions, which are sold all over the world. A "Technikum" with the latest state-of-the-art equipment is available for customers for developing or improving new products and processes. Since 1991, Glatt has been working on a series of major projects for well-known companies such as Bayer-Schering, Sanofi-Aventis, AstraZeneca, Novartis, Merck and Teva. In close cooperation with partners involved in research and development Glatt participates in the research and development of new kinds of light materials for various industries, for example motor vehicle and plant manufacturing.

Company Profile

Internationale Technik – Druckmessumformer und Drucktransmitter
International technology – Pressure measuring transducers and pressure transmitters

ADZ NAGANO GmbH

Geschäftsführer/**Managers:**
Dipl.-Ing. Dietmar Arndt
Dipl.-Ing. Wolfgang Dürfeld

Gründungsjahr/**Year of foundation:** 1998

Mitarbeiter/**Employees:** 87

Umsatz 2007/Turnover 2007:
10,7 Millionen Euro/10.7 million euros

Geschäftsfelder/**Business fields:**
Halbleiterindustrie
Automobilindustrie
Elektronik
Medizintechnik
Umwelttechnik
Semiconductor industry
Automotive industry
Electronics
Medical technology
Environmental technology

Anschrift/**Address:**
Bergener Ring 43
D-01458 Ottendorf-Okrilla
Telefon +49 (0) 35205 5969-30
Telefax +49 (0) 35205 5969-59
info@adz.de
www.adz.de

Angesiedelt am Hightech-Standort nördlich von Dresden, entwickelt und produziert die ADZ NAGANO GmbH Drucksensortechnik in Spitzenqualität.
Mit einem Team von knapp 90 engagierten Mitarbeitern hat sich das Unternehmen seit seiner Gründung zu einem international gefragten Hersteller von Druckmessumformern und Drucktransmittern entwickelt. In allen relevanten Bereichen wie Prozess-, Umwelt-, Automatisierungs- und Kfz-Technik sind wir zu Hause. Wir verfügen über exzellente Fachleute auf den Gebieten der industriellen Schaltungstechnik, Mikroelektronik, Mikro-, Aufbau- und Verbindungstechnik sowie Mikrosystemtechnik.
Unser Haupttätigkeitsfeld ist die kundenorientierte Entwicklung und Produktion von Sensoren und Sensorsystemen. Durch konsequente Erhöhung des Forschungs- und Entwicklungspotenzials sowie Erweiterung und Modernisierung der Fertigungskapazitäten konnte das Sortiment bereits auf über 4.000 produzierbare Drucktransmittertypen ausgebaut werden. Durch Einsatz modernster Technologien, sorgfältige Auswahl der Zulieferer und Umsetzung eines effizienten Qualitätssicherungssystems ist es uns nach kurzer Zeit gelungen, das Vertrauen der Kunden weltweit zu gewinnen. Dafür sprechen allein 2007 über 240.000 verkaufte Sensoren für industrielle Anwendungen.
ADZ NAGANO – See our solutions!

Resident at the high-tech location to the north of Dresden, ADZ NAGANO GmbH develops and produces pressure sensor technology of the highest quality. With a team of 90 committed employees, the enterprise has, since its foundation, developed into an internationally sought-after manufacturer of pressure measuring transducers and pressure transmitters. We are at home in all relevant areas such as process, environment, automation and automobile technology. We have first-rate professionals at our disposal in the areas of industrial circuit technology, microelectronics, micro-, structural design and coupling technology as well as microsystems engineering. Our core field of activity is the customer-oriented development and production of sensors and sensory systems. Through the consistent enhancement of research and development potential as well as the upgrading and modernization of production capacity, the assortment has already been expanded to over 4,000 producible types of pressure transmitters. We have succeeded in gaining the confidence of clients worldwide in a short period of time through the use of the most modern technologies, the careful selection of suppliers and the implementation of an efficient quality assurance system. This is supported by the sale of more than 240,000 sensors for industrial application in 2007 alone.
ADZ NAGANO – See our solutions!

Oben: Kalibrierraum
Above: Calibration room

Unten: Firmengebäude
Below: Company building

Nanoelektronik – Praxisnahe Forschung in neuen Kooperationsformen
Nanoelectronics – Practical research in new cooperation models

Prof. Dr. Peter Kücher
Der Autor hat von 1986 bis 1998 bei Siemens gewirkt, unter anderem als Projektleiter zur Entwicklung der 0,25-μm-Technologie für einen 256M DRAM. In der Zeit von 1998 bis 2005 vertrat er geschäftsführend Infineon Technologies in Dresden. Kücher ist seit 2005 Leiter des in Kooperation von AMD, Qimonda und der Fraunhofer-Gesellschaft betriebenen Centers Nanoelektronische Technologien.
The author was employed at Siemens from 1986 to 1998, amongst other things as the project leader for the development of 0,25 μm technology for a 256M DRAM. In the period from 1998 to 2005, he represented Infineon Technologies in Dresden as the managing director. Since 2005, he has been the head of the Nanoelectronic Technology Centre, organized in cooperation of AMD, Qimonda and the Fraunhofer Society.

Die Strukturgrößen in der Mikroelektronik liegen heute bereits deutlich unter 100 Nanometer und sind damit circa 1.000-mal kleiner als der Durchmesser eines menschlichen Haares. Bei Mikroprozessorchips, den „Herzen" unserer Computer, war es vor etwa fünf Jahren noch eine Spitzenleistung, 55 Millionen Transistoren auf einer Fläche von einem Quadratzentimeter unterzubringen. Heute erreichen moderne Prozessoren die drei- bis zehnfache Anzahl mit einer Taktfrequenz von über ein Gigahertz auf vergleichbarer Fläche. Durch fortschreitende Miniaturisierung der Computerchips zu immer kleineren Strukturen konnte eine erhebliche Steigerung der Performance erreicht werden. Nach einer Prognose von Gordon Moore Anfang der 70er Jahre soll sich die Leistungsfähigkeit moderner, hochintegrierter Halbleiterprodukte etwa alle zwei Jahre verdoppeln, dazu kommt eine Halbierung der Kosten pro Funktion – das ist der Schlüssel für den Erfolg der Mikroelektronik. Zunehmend erreicht man aber die physikalischen Grenzen in den Strukturbreiten und der Einsatz moderner Fertigungstechniken ist mit einem starken Anstieg der Kosten für Entwicklung und Produktion verbunden. Zudem werden die Produktlebenszyklen kürzer und die Zahl der Varianten eines Produkts, optimiert für die spezielle Anwendung, hat deutlich zugenommen. Diese Änderung in den Rahmenbedingungen erfordert auch neue Konzepte für die Zusammenarbeit von Industrie, Forschung und Entwicklung. Dresden – mit mehr als 40.000 Beschäftigten im Bereich der Elektrotechnik und als ein europäisches Zentrum der Mikroelektronik – ist ein Spiegel für unterschiedliche Forschungskonzepte.

Beispielhaft können hier das Advanced Mask Technology Center, das Fraunhofer-Center Nanoelektronische Technologien und das Nanoelectronic Materials Laboratory genannt werden. Sie fokussieren sich in ihrem jeweiligen spezifischen Forschungs- und Entwicklungsumfeld auf die schnelle Überführung von Innovationen der Nanoelektronik in wirtschaftliche Anwendungen. Mit ihrer besonderen Innovationskraft und der für Deutschland in mancher Hinsicht exemplarischen Konzeption sind sie als Pilotprojekte für Public Private-Partnerships (PPP) anzusehen und zeigen, wie impulsgebend die gesamte Vernetzung innerhalb des Forschungs- und Technologieclusters Dresden ist.

Am Fraunhofer CNT wird seit Gründung im Mai 2005 nicht nur Forschung sondern auch Kooperation großgeschrieben.

Nanoelectronics

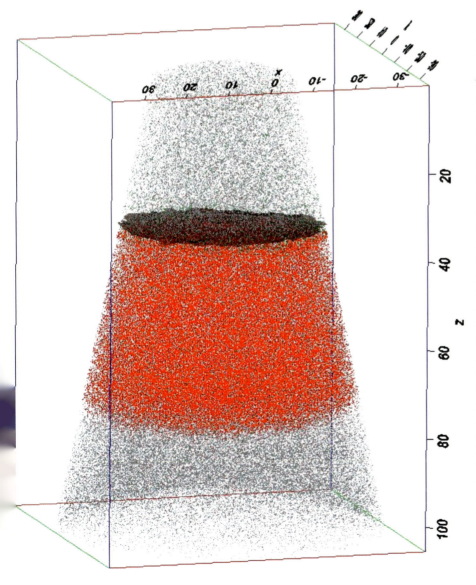

3D-Darstellung der Atomanordnung einer Materialprobe.
A 3D representation of the atomic arrangement of a material sample.

Today the structural measurements in microelectronics lie markedly below 100 nanometres and are therewith approximately 1,000 times smaller than the diameter of a human hair. In the case of microprocessor chips, the "heart" of our computers, it was still an outstanding achievement about five years ago to accommodate 55 million transistors in an area of one square centimetre. Today, modern processors achieve three to ten times the amount with a frequency over a gigahertz in a comparable area. Through the advanced miniaturization of computer chips to ever smaller structures, a substantial escalation in performance could be achieved. According to a forecast made by Gordon Moore in the early seventies, the efficiency of modern, highly integrated semiconductor products should double every two years or so and with it an additional halving of costs per function, that is the key to the success of microelectronics. One, however, increasingly reaches the physical barriers in structural breadths and the application of modern finishing technologies is linked to a heavy cost increase in development and production.

Denn zu diesem Zweck haben die Halbleiterhersteller *Qimonda* und *AMD Dresden* gemeinsam mit der *Fraunhofer-Gesellschaft* und unter Mitwirkung der Technischen Universität Dresden diese Einrichtung als PPP auf den Weg gebracht. Im Fraunhofer-Center Nanoelektronische Technologien forschen die Wissenschaftler in unmittelbarer Nähe zu den modernsten 300-Millimeter-Fertigungslinien der Industriepartner. Die 40 Anlagen auf 800 Quadratmetern Reinraum und 140 Quadratmetern Laborfläche für die Prozessentwicklung und Analytik entsprechen dabei dem letzten Stand, und Entwicklungen können unmittelbar in die Fertigungen überführt werden – entsprechend der Anforderung kurzer Innovationszyklen. Die Forschungsarbeiten konzentrieren sich auf die Kompetenzbereiche neue Materialien, Metrologie und Analytik, innovative Prozesse, Strukturierung sowie Devices und Integration. Zum Beispiel arbeiten hier Wissenschaftler an einem Analysegerät (LEAP, local electron atomic probe), das es ermöglicht, den Materialaufbau auf atomarer Ebene in einer 3D-Darstellung zu analysieren. So können die Wissenschaftler feststellen, wie sich einzelne Atome einer Schicht nach unterschiedlichen Prozessierungsschritten, wie nach deren Abscheidung und Temperaturbehandlung, verhalten, welche Fremdatome eindiffundiert sind und ob eine Sperrschicht auch „dicht" ist – ein solches Tool ist derzeit einzigartig in Europa.

Auf die Erforschung von Materialien mit bisher noch unbekannten Eigenschaften hat sich in Dresden das Nanoelectronic Materials Laboratory, kurz NaMLab, spezialisiert. Auch diese Einrichtung ist eine Kooperation, hier der TU Dresden und der *Qimonda Dresden GmbH & Co. OHG*, in Form einer gemeinnützigen GmbH, die seit 2007 besteht. Speicherprodukte der Zukunft erfordern neue Materialien und funktionale Schichten, die heute noch nicht für die Produktion tauglich sind. Neben der Grundlagenforschung arbeiten die Wissenschaftler am NaMLab auch an der Charakterisierung dieser Schichten, um deren Potenzial für eine mögliche Integration in die Fertigung von Halbleiterprodukten für Dimensionen von unter 30 Nanometern auszuarbeiten. Neben den Wissenschaftlern, die in die Projekte einbezogen sind, entsteht hier eine einzigartige Möglichkeit, auch junge Studenten und Talente der Technischen Universität schon frühzeitig in Projekte einzubinden.

Die *Advanced Mask Technology Center GmbH & Co. KG* (AMTC) ist ein Joint Venture von *AMD Inc.*, *Qimonda* und *Toppan Photomasks Inc.* Bei der Gründung im Jahre 2002 entstand ein führendes Zentrum für Forschung und Entwicklung sowie Pilotproduktion von Fotolithografiemasken der jeweils neuesten Generation für Prozessoren und Speicher. Fotomasken bestehen aus hochreinen Glasscheiben, auf denen präzise Abbildungen der integrierten Schaltkreise (oder Halbleiterchips) jeweils für eine Ebene aktiver Elemente wie Transistoren und Speicher sowie für die Verdrahtung der Schaltkreise dargestellt werden.

Nanoelectronics

Wissenschaftler bei Arbeiten an Anlagen im Reinraum des Fraunhofer CNT.
Scientists at work on equipment in the clean room of the Fraunhofer CNT.

In addition, the product life cycles become shorter and the amount of variation of a product, optimized for the specific application, has clearly increased. These changes in the basic conditions also necessitate new concepts for collaboration of industry, research and development. Dresden – with more than 40,000 employees in the field of electro-technology and as a European centre of microelectronics – is a looking glass for a variety of research concepts.

By way of example, the Advanced Mask Technology Center, the Fraunhofer Center Nanoelectronic Technologies (Fraunhofer CNT) and the Nanoelectronic Materials Laboratory may be mentioned. In their respective specific research and development environments, they are focused on the rapid transformation of nanoelectronic innovations into commercial applications. With their special innovative energy and in some respects exemplary conceptions, they are to be considered as pilot projects for public-private partnerships (PPP) and show how invigorating the entire networking is within Dresden's research and technology cluster.

At the Fraunhofer CNT, not only research but also cooperation has been a priority since its foundation in May 2005.

For this purpose, the semiconductor producer *Qimonda* and *AMD Dresden*, together with the *Fraunhofer Society* and with the participation of the Dresden University of Technology, have put this establishment on the right path as a PPP. In the Fraunhofer Center Nanoelectronic Technologies, scientists do research in close proximity to industry partners with most modern 300-millimeter production lines. The 40 facilities in an 800-square-metre clean room area and 140 square metres of laboratory space for process development and analytics correspond to the status quo, and developments can immediately be transferred to the manufacturing process – according to the requirements of shorter innovation cycles. Research work is concentrated on the competence fields of new materials, metrology and analytics, innovative processes, structuring as well as devices and integration. Scientists here, for instance, are working on an analysis device (LEAP, local electron atomic probe) that allows for the analysis of material structure on atomic level in a 3D presentation. In this way scientists can determine how individual atoms behave in a layer after different processing steps, how they behave after their separation and temperature treatment, which foreign atoms are diffused and whether a barrier layer is also "airtight" – such a tool is currently one of a kind in Europe.

In Dresden, the Nanoelectronics Materials Laboratory (NaMLab) has specialized itself in the exploration of materials with hitherto unknown characteristics.

Standort des Fraunhofer CNT auf dem Betriebsgelände von Infineon und Qimonda in Dresden.
The location of the Fraunhofer CNT on the business premises of Infineon and Qimonda in Dresden.

Die Masken dienen als Vorlage im optischen Abbildungsprozess für die Erstellung der integrierten Schaltkreise auf Siliziumscheiben. Die Abbildung erfolgt auf fotoempfindlichem Lack, der entwickelt wird und dann wiederum als Maske für die zu ätzenden Strukturen dient. Durch eine mehrfache Wiederholung der Lithografieprozesse entstehen sozusagen die Pläne für die Herstellung der Schaltkreise. Komplexe Schaltkreise erfordern bis zu 60 Maskenschritte, von denen jeder eine eigene Fotomaske benötigt. Einer der Schwerpunkte der wissenschaftlichen Arbeiten am AMTC liegt auf der Entwicklung von Reticle-Enhancement-Technologien. Masken mit dieser Technologie erlauben es, Strukturen auf dem Wafer zu erzeugen, die unterhalb der Wellenlänge des Lichts im Belichtungsgerät liegen. Dabei werden für den Herstellungsprozess der Fotomaske unter anderem Verfahren wie Elektronenstrahl- und Laserschreiben, Fotolack-Entwicklung, Trockenätzen, Optische Atomic Force Mikroskopie und hochauflösende Rasterelektronenmikroskopie eingesetzt.

Was ist diesen drei Unternehmen gemeinsam? Sie erzielen hervorragende Ergebnisse in der Hochtechnologieforschung durch Kooperation. Alle Mitarbeiter entwickeln vor Ort eng mit den Experten der Partnerunternehmen sowie mit Wissenschaftlern verschiedener Forschungs- und Hochschuleinrichtungen zusammen. Das ermöglicht eine hohe Effizienz in der Nutzung der benötigten Geräte, Synergieeffekte und die Möglichkeit des „Lernens von Anderen". Weiterhin können gewonnene Erkenntnisse schneller und kostengünstiger in die Fertigung umgesetzt werden.

In Anbetracht der kurzen Produktzyklen ist es das große Ziel der Hersteller, die Fertigung weiter zu optimieren. Dabei sollen Fertigungszeiten verkürzt sowie Produktvielfalt und Leistungsfähigkeit erhöht werden. Das kommt auch dem Anwender zugute. Am Ende der Forschungs- und Produktionsprozesse entstehen für den Kunden bessere, schnellere und kostengünstiger Produkte. Durch mehr Vielfalt und Energieeffizienz läutet die neue Generation der Produkte eine weitere Stufe des „Erlebens" beim Kunden ein.

Auch Bund und Länder haben ein starkes Interesse am Fortschritt der Kenntnisse auf dem Bereich der Nanoelektronik. So werden alle hier genannten Beispiele unterstützt vom Bundesministerium für Bildung und Forschung (BMBF), dem Land Sachsen sowie der Europäischen Union.

This establishment is also a cooperation, of the TU Dresden and the *Qimonda Dresden GmbH & Co. OHG*, in the form of a non-profit limited company, which has been in existence since 2007. Storage products of the future necessitate new materials and functional layers, which are not yet suitable for production today. In addition to basic research, scientists at NaMLab are working on the characterization of these layers in order to calculate their potential for possible integration into the production of semiconductor products for dimensions below 30 nanometres. In addition to scientists included in projects, a unique opportunity exists here for the early involvement of young students and the talents of the University of Technology in projects.

The *Advanced Mask Technology Center GmbH & Co. KG* (AMTC) is a joint venture between *AMD Inc.*, *Qimonda* and *Toppan Photomasks Inc*. With their foundation in 2002, a leading centre for research and development as well as for pilot production of photolithography masks of the respective latest generation of processors and storage devices was created. Photo masks consist of high-purity glass panes on which precision images of integrated circuits (or semiconductor chips) are illustrated, each for a level of active elements such as transistors and storage as well as for the wiring of circuits.

The masks serve as a template in the optical imaging process for the design capture of integrated circuits on silicon wafers. The image is carried out on photo-sensitive lacquer, which is developed and which then again serves as a mask for the structures to be etched. Through a multiple repetition of the lithography process, the plans for the production of the circuits are generated. Complex circuits necessitate up to 60 mask steps, in which each requires its own photomask. One of the focal points of the scientific work at AMTC lies in the development of reticle enhancement technologies. Masks containing this technology allow for structures which lie below the wave length of the light in the exposure unit, to be created on the wafers. Thereby, for the production process of photomasks, amongst other things, processes such as electronic beam and laser writing, photoresist development, dry etching, optical atomic force microscopy and high-resolution scanning electron microscopy are applied.

What do these three organizations have in common? They achieve outstanding results in high technology research through cooperation. All employees develop on site closely together with the experts of partner organizations as well as with scientists of different research and university institutions. This allows for elevated efficiency in the utilization of the required equipment, synergy effects and the opportunity of "learning from others". Furthermore, obtained findings can be implemented into production faster and cheaper.

In view of short production cycles, it is the ultimate objective of producers to further optimize the manufacturing process. Thereby manufacturing times should be shortened and product diversity and efficiency be increased. That also benefits the user. At the end of the research and production processes, better, faster and cheaper products are generated for the client. Through more diversity and energy-efficiency, the new generation of products heralds the start of another level of "experience" for clients.

Also the Federal Government and the states have a vested interest in the advancement of knowledge in the field of nanoelectronics. Thus, all the examples mentioned here are supported by the Federal Ministry of Education and Research (BMBF), the state of Saxony as well as the European Union.

Brücken bauen – Synergien nutzen
Building bridges – Capitalizing on synergies

PSE 2008, Konferenzteilnehmer vor dem Kongresshaus in Garmisch-Partenkirchen.
PSE 2008, conference participants in front of the Kongresshaus in Garmisch-Partenkirchen.

Die zentrale Aufgabe der EFDS besteht in der Förderung einer engen Zusammenarbeit zwischen Unternehmen und Institutionen, die auf dem Gebiet der Materialentwicklung, des Anlagenbaus, der Lohnbehandlung und der Oberflächencharakterisierung tätig sind, und den Anwenderbranchen in der Industrie. Die EFDS ist ein eingetragener Verein der Branche der Vakuum- und Plasmaoberflächentechnik und wurde 1992 in Dresden gegründet. Der Verein hat derzeit 170 Mitglieder – Unternehmen des Anlagenbaus und der Lohnbeschichtung, Institutionen, Einrichtungen und Privatpersonen überwiegend aus Deutschland aber auch aus Belgien, Dänemark, Frankreich, Griechenland, Liechtenstein, den Niederlanden, Österreich, Schweiz und den USA.

Hauptaktivitäten
- Beantragung der finanziellen Förderung und Betreuung von Projekten der industriellen Gemeinschaftsforschung
- Projekt- und Netzwerkmanagement, zum Beispiel im Rahmen von NEMO-Projekten über AiF/BMWi
- Beratung zu Fragen der Oberflächentechnik, vor allem zu innovativen Verfahren der Vakuum- und Plasmaoberflächenbehandlung
- Vermittlung von kompetenten Lohnbeschichtern und Anlagenbaufirmen sowie Organisation von Musterbeschichtungen
- Beratung zur Unternehmensführung
- Erarbeitung von Gutachten und Studien zu neuen Produkten, Märkten und Investitionsvorhaben sowie Erarbeitung von Strategieempfehlungen
- Vertretung der EFDS und ihrer Mitgliedsfirmen und -einrichtungen auf Messen
- Organisation von Konferenzen, Workshops und Industrieausstellungen, Anwenderforen und Ähnlichem mehr

Die EFDS hat seit 2005 die Geschäftsführung des Arbeitskreises Plasmaoberflächentechnologie inne. Damit verbunden ist die Organisation und Durchführung der internationalen Tagung „Plasma Surface Engineering-PSE" im zweijährigen Rhythmus. Die 11. PSE fand vom 15.–19.09.2008 mit hoher internationaler Beteiligung in Garmisch-Partenkirchen statt, die 12. PSE ist für den 13.–17.09.2010 geplant. Ein weiteres Highlight ist die Veranstaltungsreihe „Industrieausstellung & Workshop-Woche Vakuumbeschichtung und Plasmaoberflächentechnik", die ebenfalls im zweijährigen Rhythmus durchgeführt wird und als V2009 vom 20.–22.10.2009 in Dresden avisiert ist.

Die EFDS ist unter anderem Mitglied im Netzwerk SILICON SAXONY eV und organisiert Technologietransferveranstaltungen für vor allem sächsische Unternehmen und Einrichtungen.

Company Profile

Sitz der EFDS-Geschäftsstelle im TechnologieZentrumDresden.
The EFDS registered office in the Dresden Technology Center.

Europäische Forschungsgesellschaft Dünne Schichten eV

Vorstandsvorsitzender/CEO:
Dr. Andreas Mucha

Geschäftsführer/Managing Director:
Dr. Frank Böger

Gründungsjahr/Year of foundation:
1992

Mitarbeiter/Employees:
6   Geschäftsstelle
170 Mitgliederstand 01.01.2009
6   office
170 membership status 01.01.2009

Geschäftsfelder/Business activities:
- Anlagenbau
- Beratung
- Technologietransfer
- Beschichtung
- Oberflächenbeschichtung
- Vakuumbeschichten
- Plasmaoberflächentechnik
- Dünne Schichten
- Vakuumtechnik
- Workshops, Konferenzen
- Industrieausstellungen
- Industrielle Gemeinschaftsforschung
- Plant engineering and construction
- Consulting
- Technology transfer
- Coating
- Surface coating
- Vacuum coating
- Plasma surface engineering
- Thin films
- Vacuum equipment
- Workshops, Conferences
- Industry exhibitions
- Industrial joint research

Anschrift/Address:
Gostritzer Straße 63
D-01217 Dresden
Telefon +49 (0) 351 8718-370
Telefax +49 (0) 351 8718-431
tos@efds.org
www.efds.org

The main task of EFDS (European Society of Thin Films) is to promote close collaboration between organizations and institutions that operate on the fields of material development, plant engineering, subcontract treatment services and surface characterization as well as the consumer sectors in the industry. Founded in Dresden in 1992, EFDS is a registered association of the vacuum and plasma surface technology industry and currently has 170 members – plant construction and job-coater organizations, institutions, establishments and private individuals, mostly from Germany, but also from Belgium, Denmark, France, Greece, Liechtenstein, the Netherlands, Austria, Switzerland and the USA.

Core activities
- The application of financial advancements and supervision of industrial joint research projects
- Project and network management, for example NEMO projects in cooperation with the AiF/BMWi
- Consultation regarding surface technology issues, particularly innovative processes of vacuum and plasma surface treatment
- Placement of competent job-coater organizations and plant construction companies as well as the organization of sample coating
- Consultation for enterprise management
- Drafting of approval certificates and surveys of new projects, markets and investment plans as well as the formulation of policy recommendations
- Representation of EFDS and its member organizations at trade fairs
- Organization of conferences, workshops and industry exhibitions, consumer forums and similar events

EFDS has held the position of management of the plasma surface technology research group since 2005. Associated therewith is the organization and implementation of the international congress "Plasma Surface Engineering-PSE" on a two-yearly basis. The 11. PSE congress took place from 15.–19.09.2008 with great international participation in Garmisch-Partenkirchen; the 12. PSE is planned for the 13.–17.09.2010. A further highlight is the event series "Industrieausstellung & Workshop-Woche Vakuumbeschichtung und Plasmaoberflächentechnik", which will likewise be carried out on a two-yearly basis the V2009 is scheduled for 20.– 22.10.2008 in Dresden.

Amongst others things, EFDS is a member of the SILICON SAXONY eV network and organizes technology-transfer events, particularly for Saxon organizations and establishments.

Hier stimmt die Mischung – Ideale Verhältnisse für Metall und Elektro
Here the mixture is right – Ideal conditions for metal and electrics

Dipl.-Ing. Andreas Huhn

Der Autor hat an der TU Dresden Maschinenbau studiert. Seit 2003 steht er an der Spitze des größten sächsischen Industrieverbandes Sachsenmetall. Bereits 1994 zählte Huhn zu den Gründern des Allgemeinen Arbeitgeberverbandes Sachsen, heute unter dem Dach von Sachsenmetall. Huhn ist geschäftsführender Gesellschafter der auf emaillierte Paneele spezialisierten Omeras GmbH in Lauter bei Aue.

The author studied mechanical engineering at the Dresden University of Technology. Since 2003, he has been the head of the largest Saxon industrial association, Sachsenmetall. Already in 1994, Mr Huhn was one of the founders of the Allgemeiner Arbeitgeberverband Sachsen, which today is under the umbrella of Sachsenmetall. He is the managing partner of Omeras GmbH, which specializes in enamelled panels, in Lauter near Aue.

Die sächsische Landeshauptstadt Dresden zählt mit den angrenzenden Städten Meißen, Radebeul, Freital und Pirna zu den wirtschaftlich führenden Regionen im Freistaat Sachsen. Das Gebiet zwischen dem Elbsandsteingebirge und der Porzellanstadt Meißen kann dabei auf eine großartige Industriegeschichte zurückblicken. Beispielsweise wurde im damals noch vor den Grenzen Dresdens liegenden Stadtteil Übigau 1837 das erste Personendampfschiff für die Oberelbe gebaut, zwei Jahre später dann die erste deutsche Dampflokomotive, die legendäre „Saxonia". Im Jahr 1900 stellte Emil Nacke in Coswig das erste sächsische Automobil vor, 1905 nahm er auch die Fertigung von Lkw auf.

Während in der 1921 gegründeten Stadt Freital schon seit Mitte des 19. Jahrhunderts ein Stahlwerk ansässig ist, befand sich in Dresden im 20. Jahrhundert zum Beispiel das Zentrum der Fotoapparate- und Kinogeräteindustrie. Hier wurden in den 1930er Jahren die ersten einäugigen Spiegelreflexkameras gebaut, aber auch der erste Fernseher von Manfred von Ardenne. Der Name der kleinen Stadt Glashütte im Osterzgebirge vor den Toren Dresdens steht für Armbanduhren mit Qualität von Weltruf. Anfang der 1960er Jahre wurde dann mit der Gründung des Zentrums Mikroelektronik Dresden (ZMD) und des Kombinats Robotron der Grundstein für den Mikroelektronikstandort Dresden gelegt.

Aufbauend auf dieser vielseitigen Erfolgsgeschichte konnte die Region Dresden nach dem Mauerfall an ihre Tradition anknüpfen und gleichzeitig neue Industriebereiche erschließen. Von den heute 1.500 Betrieben der sächsischen Metall- und Elektroindustrie haben in der Landeshauptstadt rund 200 Firmen ihren Sitz, die über 20.000 Mitarbeiter beschäftigen. Daran partizipieren zusätzlich zahlreiche Dienstleister und Zulieferer.

In Dresden stimmt die Mischung. Traditionelle Wirtschaftsbereiche nehmen einen festen Platz ein neben den Neuansiedlungen der Hightech-Industrie. Wichtige Wachstums- und Entwicklungsimpulse gehen dabei nicht nur von der Mikroelektronik aus, in die seit den 1990er Jahren mehr als zwölf Milliarden Euro investiert wurden, sondern auch von einem hochinnovativen Maschinen- und Anlagenbau und einer wettbewerbsfähigen Luftfahrtindustrie. Auch die Solarindustrie hat sich in der Dresdner Region fest etabliert und sorgt dafür, dass moderne Technologien zur Energiegewinnung von hier aus in die ganze Welt exportiert werden.

Metal and Electrical Industry 75

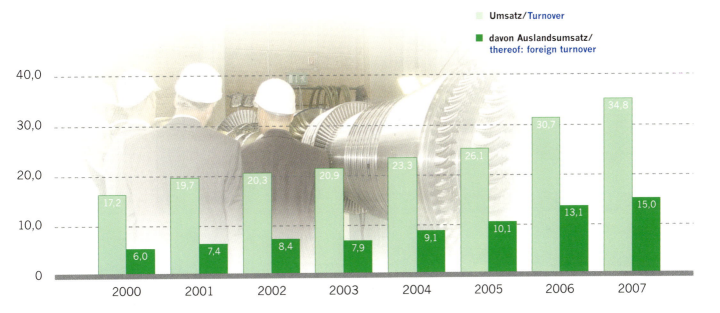

Umsatz in der sächsischen Metall- und Elektroindustrie in Milliarden Euro.
Turnover in the Saxon metal and electrical industry in billion euros.

The Saxon state capital of Dresden, with the adjoining cities of Meißen, Radebeul, Freital and Pirna, counts among the leading economic regions in the Free State of Saxony. The area between the Elbe Sandstone Mountains and the porcelain city of Meißen is able to look back upon a magnificent industrial history. For instance, the first passenger steamship was built in 1837 for the upper Elbe river in the Übigau city quarter, which at that time still lay outside the Dresden city limit. Two years later, the first German steam locomotive, the legendary "Saxonia", was also built there. In 1900, Emil Nacke introduced the first Saxon motor car in Coswig, and in 1905 he also took up the production of motor trucks.

In the city of Freital, established in 1921, a steel mill was already located since the middle of the 19th century, whereas in Dresden for instance the centre of the camera and cinema equipment industry was situated in the 20th century. Here, in the 1930s the first monocular reflex camera was built, and also the first television by Manfred von Ardenne. The name of the small town of Glashütte, in the eastern Erz Mountains in front of Dresden's gates, is known for wrist watches with an international reputation for quality. The cornerstone for the Dresden microelectronics location was laid at the beginning of the 1960s through the establishment of the Microelectronic Center Dresden (ZMD) and the Robotron enterprise (VEB Kombinat Robotron).

Based on this varied success story, the Dresden region could live up to its tradition after the fall of the Berlin Wall and simultaneously develop new industrial sectors. Of the 1,500 enterprises operating in the Saxon metal and electrical industry today, around 200 firms are based in the state capital, employing more than 20,000 people. In addition, numerous service providers and suppliers participate there.

Metall- und Elektroindustrie

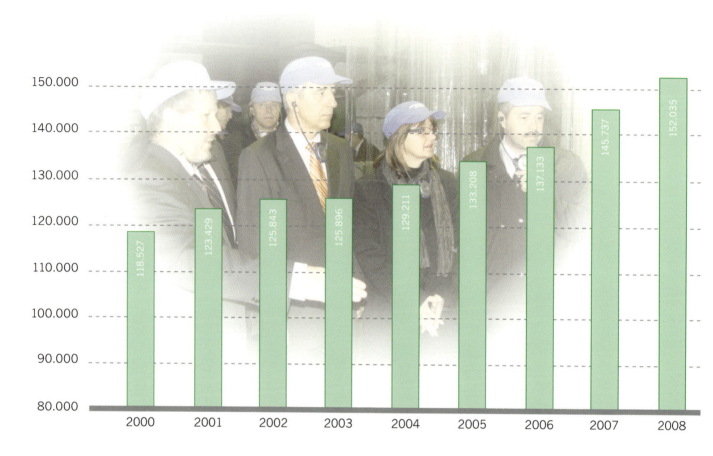

Beschäftigte in der sächsischen Metall- und Elektroindustrie.
Employees of the Saxon metal and electrical industry.

2000: 118.527
2001: 123.429
2002: 125.843
2003: 125.896
2004: 129.211
2005: 133.208
2006: 137.133
2007: 145.737
2008: 152.035

Aktuell sind allein in Dresden über 80 Unternehmen im Maschinen- und Anlagenbau tätig. Sie beschäftigen mehr als 5.100 Mitarbeiter und haben einen Exportanteil von über 40 Prozent. Dabei liegt der Schwerpunkt auf Spezial- und Sondermaschinen, zum Beispiel für die Verpackungsindustrie, aber auch auf der Antriebs- und Prüftechnik.

Als 1811 in Dresden eine Frau mit einem Ballonflug den Grundstein der Luftfahrt legte, war noch nicht zu erahnen, dass hier fast 200 Jahre später ein wichtiger Spezialanbieter der Flugzeugindustrie angesiedelt sein würde. Die Elbe Flugzeugwerke sind heute mit ihrer Umrüstung von Passagiermaschinen zu Frachtern ein beredtes Beispiel für die vielen Unternehmen, die, ihre Tradition nutzend, aus Dresden einen innovativen, dynamisch wachsenden Wirtschaftsstandort machen.

Für die Dresdner Metall- und Elektroindustrie ist die Nähe und damit der direkte Kontakt zur Forschung ein wichtiger Standortvorteil. Neben der Technischen Universität haben sich in der sächsischen Landeshauptstadt verschiedene Forschungseinrichtungen wie Fraunhofer-Institute, die Max-Planck-Gesellschaft oder Institute der Leibniz-Gemeinschaft angesiedelt und knüpfen mit ihren Innovationen an den Erfindergeist der Region an.

Aber Dresden und sein Umfeld sind auch ein Magnet für Fachkräfte aus nah und fern. Eine hohe Bildungsqualität, interessante Berufschancen und ein lebenswertes Umfeld mit vielfältigen Angeboten aus Kultur, Sport und Freizeit machen Dresden zu einem Anziehungspunkt.

Es ist ohne Zweifel die Mischung aus Kultur und Wissenschaft, aus Hightech und Tradition, Lebensqualität und Geschäftstüchtigkeit, die den Erfolg Dresdens ausmacht. 2008 wurde die sächsische Landeshauptstadt im Städtevergleich der Initiative Neue Soziale Marktwirtschaft und der WirtschaftsWoche erneut zur dynamischsten Stadt Deutschlands gewählt, weil sich hier die wirtschaftlichen Bedingungen in den letzten fünf Jahren am besten entwickelt haben.

Die sächsische Metall- und Elektroindustrie hat in Dresden ein bedeutendes Zentrum, das einen wesentlichen Beitrag zum Wachstum dieses Sektors in ganz Sachsen leistet.

Metal and Electrical Industry

Elbe Flugzeugwerke Dresden: Nach Umrüstung hebt ein Airbus für Emirates SkyCargo ab.
The Elbe Flugzeugwerke Dresden: After conversion, an Airbus takes off for Emirates SkyCargo.

In Dresden the mixture is right. Traditional economic sectors take up a steady position alongside the new settlements of the high-tech industry. Not only do important growth and development impulses spring from microelectronics, where more than twelve billion euros have been invested since the 1990s, but also from a highly innovative mechanical and plant engineering industry and a competitive aircraft industry. The solar industry has also established itself firmly in the Dresden region and it ensures the exportation of modern technologies for energy generation from here to the whole world.

Currently more than 80 organizations in the mechanical and plant engineering sector operate in Dresden alone. They employ more than 5,100 people and have an export ratio of over 40 per cent. The focal point lies in special and specialized machinery such as for the packaging industry, however also in drive and test engineering.

When a woman laid the cornerstone for aviation with a balloon flight in Dresden in 1811, it was not yet to be anticipated that, almost 200 years later, an important specialist supplier of the aircraft industry would be settled here. The Elbe Flugzeugwerke (aircraft works), with its conversion of passenger aircraft to freighter, is an eloquent example of the many organizations which, utilizing their traditions, turn Dresden into an innovative, dynamically growing economic region.

For the Dresden metal and electrical industry, the close proximity, and therewith the direct contact, with research is an important location advantage. In addition to the University of Technology, a variety of research institutions in the Saxon state capital – such as the Fraunhofer Institutes, the Max Planck Society or the Leibniz Association – have settled in the region and with their innovations live up to the inventive talent of the region.

Dresden and its surroundings are however also a magnet for qualified personnel from near and far. A high quality of education, interesting career opportunities and a liveable environment with a versatile range of offers of cultural, sport and leisure time activities, make Dresden a centre of attraction.

It is without a doubt the mixture between culture and science, between high-tech and tradition, quality of life and salesmanship that characterizes Dresden's success. The Saxon state capital was again voted as the most dynamic city in Germany in a city comparison in 2008 by the Initiative Neue Soziale Marktwirtschaft (New Social Market Economy Initiative) and the Wirtschaftswoche (business magazine). This is because the economic conditions have developed here very well in the last five years.

The Saxon metal and electrical industry has a significant centre in Dresden, which makes a considerable contribution to the growth of this sector throughout Saxony.

Maschinen- und Anlagenbau

Region für die Zukunft gut gerüstet
A region well-equipped for the future

Prof. Dr.-Ing. Dieter Weidlich
Der 1952 geborene Autor hat an der TH Chemnitz Maschinenbau studiert, wurde 1982 promoviert und 2002 von der TU Chemnitz zum außerplanmäßigen Professor ernannt. Er hat unter anderem als Oberingenieur am Fraunhofer-Institut für Werkzeugmaschinen und Umformtechnik gewirkt. Prof. Weidlich ist seit April 2009 Projektmanager bei der Verbundinitiative Maschinenbau Sachsen VEMAS.

The author was born in 1952 and studied mechanical engineering at the Chemnitz University of Technology (TU). In 1982 he was awarded his doctorate and in 2002, was appointed extracurricular professor at the TU Chemnitz. He worked as chief engineer at the Fraunhofer Institute for Machine Tools and Forming Technology. Since April 2009, Prof. Weidlich has been the project manager at the Verbundinitiative Maschinenbau Sachsen VEMAS.

In Sachsen hat der Maschinenbau eine lange Tradition. Das Land gilt gemeinhin als Wiege der Branche. Bereits 1703 gründete Johann Esche in Limbach die erste deutsche Fabrik für Spezialmaschinen der Textilindustrie. Auch der deutsche Werkzeugmaschinenbau hat in Sachsen seine Wurzeln. Aus Sachsen stammen der erste maschinelle Tuchwebstuhl der Welt, die erste deutsche Farbdruckschnellpresse oder die Nähwirktechnik.

Heute sind mehr als 38.000 Menschen im sächsischen Maschinenbau beschäftigt und die Unternehmen der Branche setzen mehr als sechs Milliarden Euro um.

Die Region Dresden
Im östlichen Sachsen, in der Region Dresden, sind gerade die Bereiche Forschung und Entwicklung ein echtes Schwergewicht. Von der Technischen Universität Dresden und der Hochschule für Technik und Wirtschaft in Dresden über die Hochschule Zittau/Görlitz bis hin zu der bundesweit einzigartigen Konzentration diverser Forschungsinstitute der Fraunhofer-Gesellschaft, der Max-Planck-Gesellschaft und der Leibniz-Gemeinschaft – im Verbund mit der bestehenden Wirtschaft erweist sich diese Forschungs- und Entwicklungslandschaft in der Region Dresden auch auf lange Sicht als ausgesprochen zukunftsfähig.

In der Region Dresden und Ostsachsen zeichnet sich die Unternehmens-Landschaft für Maschinen- und Anlagenbau neben der Forschung
– in Dresden durch die Kompetenzfelder
• Sondermaschinen,
• Automatisierungstechnik,
• Druckmaschinen,
• Anlagenbau sowie
• Nahrungsmittel- und
• Verpackungsmaschinen

– in Görlitz/Zittau durch die Kompetenzfelder
• Sondermaschinen,
• Automatisierungstechnik sowie
• Werkzeugmaschinen- und Formenbau
aus.

Exzellente Beispiele für marktführende Unternehmen lassen sich in vielen Bereichen des modernen Maschinen- und Anlagenbaus aufzählen.
So produziert *Trumpf Sachsen GmbH* mit seinen 400 Mitarbeitern Hochleistungslaserschneidmaschinen. Das Unternehmen ist einer der renommiertesten Werkzeugmaschinenhersteller in Sachsen und steht für Automatisierungskomponenten und Laserschneidmaschinen. In der Kombination Sondermaschinenbau und Automatisierungstechnik ist wiederum die *Siemens AG* der bekannteste Hersteller. *Siemens* Görlitz liefert weltweit und marktführend Dampfturbinen bis 150 Megawatt.

Mechanical and Plant Engineering

Trumpf Sachsen.
Trumpf Sachsen.

Mittelstandsauszeichnung für von Ardenne.
Medium-sized business sector award for von Ardenne.

Trumpf Hochgeschwindigkeits-Laserschneidemaschine.
Trumpf high-speed laser cutting machine.

Mechanical engineering has a long tradition in Saxony. The territory is commonly believed to be the cradle of the industrial sector. Already in 1703, Johann Esche founded the first German factory for specialized machinery for the textile industry in Limbach. The German machine tool manufacturing industry also has its roots in Saxony. The first mechanical cloth weaving loom in the world, the first German high-speed colour press and sewing mechanism technology – all stem from Saxony. Today, more than 38,000 people are employed in mechanical engineering in Saxony and the organizations in the sector transact business of more than six billion euros.

The Dresden region

In the Dresden region in eastern Saxony, there is a genuine focus, especially on the fields of research and development. From the Dresden University of Technology and the University of Applied Sciences in Dresden to the Zittau/Görlitz University of Applied Sciences right up to the nation-wide unique concentration of diverse research institutions of the Fraunhofer Society, the Max Planck Society and the Leibniz Association – in combination with the existing economy, this research and development landscape in the Dresden region proves itself to be absolutely sustainable also in the long term. In the Dresden and East Saxony region, the organizational landscape for mechanical and plant engineering distinguishes itself, in addition to research

– in Dresden in the following specialized areas:
• specialized machinery
• automation technology
• printing presses
• plant engineering as well as
• foodstuff- and
• packaging machines

– in Görlitz/Zittau in the following specialized areas:
• specialized machinery
• automation technology as well as
• machine tools and forming technology.

Excellent examples of market-leading organizations can be found in many of the modern mechanical and plant engineering spheres.

For instance, *Trumpf Sachsen* GmbH with its 400 employees produces high performance laser cutting machines. The organization is one of the most prestigious machine tool producers in Saxony and stands for automated components and laser cutting machines.

Maschinen- und Anlagenbau

Fraunhofer-Institut für Werkzeugmaschinen und Umformtechnik, Dresden.
Fraunhofer Institute for Machine Tools and Forming Technology, Dresden.

Vollautomatischer Druckplattenwechsel an einer Rapida-Bogenoffsetmaschine.
Fully-automated printing plate replacement on a Rapida sheet-fed offset press.

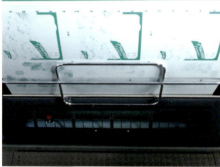

In Dresden befindet sich zudem das Kompetenzzentrum des Konzerns für Mittelleistungstransformatoren.

Sondermaschinen für den Bereich Automatisierung produziert in Dresden darüber hinaus die Firma *XENON Automatisierungstechnik GmbH*. Im Anlagenbau sind die Unternehmen *Linde-KCA-Dresden* und *von Ardenne* zu nennen.

Auf dem Gebiet des Druckmaschinenbaus ist die *Koenig & Bauer AG* mit Sitz in Radebeul der Technologieführer für wasserlose Offsetdruckmaschinen.
Als beispielhafte Spezialisten für Nahrungsmittel- und Verpackungsmaschinen sind etwa die *Glatt Systemtechnik GmbH* und *Theegarten-Pactec GmbH & Co. KG*, beide mit Sitz in Dresden, zu nennen. Der Wirtschaftssektor ist am Standort vielseitig und kann – über alle politischen Systeme hinweg – auf eine lange Erfahrung verweisen.

Internationaler Wettbewerb
Damit neue Marktchancen erkannt und genutzt werden, Innovationen in Produkt und Prozess angeboten und Wirtschaftlichkeitsreserven erschlossen werden, hat der Freistaat Sachsen die Verbundinitiative Maschinenbau Sachsen (VEMAS) ins Leben gerufen. Die VEMAS führt die Kompetenzfelder zu Unternehmensnetzwerken und Technologieprojekten zusammen. So können Forschung und Entwicklung vorangebracht und innovative Systemlösungen dem globalen Markt angeboten werden.
Die VEMAS ist seit 2003 im Auftrag des Sächsischen Staatsministeriums für Wirtschaft und Arbeit tätig und wird vom Fraunhofer Institut für Werkzeugmaschinen und Umformtechnik (IWU) geführt. Industrielle Unterstützung erfährt die Initiative durch das Kompetenzzentrum Maschinenbau Chemnitz/Sachsen eV.

Kernaufgaben der Verbundinitiative sind die Verbesserung der Innovationskraft der Unternehmen durch Technologietransfer, die Initiierung von Kooperationsprojekten, die Unterstützung bei der Erschließung neuer Märkte sowie die Gewinnung und Sicherung von hochqualifizierten Fachkräften. Für den Ausbau von Innovationskraft und Leistungsfähigkeit der sächsischen KMU zielen die Aktivitäten der VEMAS auf die nachhaltige Zusammenarbeit zwischen Wissenschaft und Wirtschaft.

Im Jahr 2009 organisierte die VEMAS dazu bereits zum zweiten Mal einen Gemeinschaftsstand zur Messe intec in Leipzig unter dem Thema „Treffpunkt Industrie und Wissenschaft". Auch die Durchführung von themenspezifischen Workshops und die Initiierung und Begleitung von Kooperationsprojekten führten in dem Jahr zu einer weiteren Stärkung der technologischen Kompetenz der Unternehmen.
Der Fokus bei der Erschließung neuer Märkte ist vor allem auf die Länder Russland und Indien gerichtet. Neben der Begleitung der sächsischen Unternehmen in den Zielmärkten vor Ort trägt auch die Betreuung von ausländischen Delegationen in Sachsen zur Anbahnung konkreter Kooperationsvorhaben bei.

Ausblick
Die globale Finanzmarktkrise mag vielen Wirtschaftsbereichen zusetzen. Langfristiger Erfolg ist aber jenen beschieden, die auf Innovation setzen. Das forschungsintensive Umfeld in der Region Dresden ist dabei für den Maschinenbau in der Region und in ganz Sachsen ein Garant für unternehmerischen Erfolg und damit langfristig auch für Wachstum und Beschäftigung.
Investoren sind in und mit Sachsen gut beraten. Maschinenbau – natürlich Sachsen!

Kontakt/Contact:

www.vemas-sachsen.de

Mechanical and Plant Engineering 81

Vollautomatische Stapellogistik an einer KBA-Druckmaschine.
Fully-automated stacking logistics on a KBA printing press.

Koenig & Bauer in Radebeul ist spezialisiert auf Bogenoffsetmaschinen für den Akzidenz- und Verpackungsdruck.
Koenig und Bauer in Radebeul is specialized in sheet-fed offset presses for job-printing and package printing.

On the other hand, in the specialized machine engineering and automation technology combination, the *Siemens AG* is the most well-known producer. Siemens Görlitz is a worldwide deliverer of and market-leader in steam turbines up to 150 megawatts.
In addition, the group's competence centre of medium-capacity transformers is found in Dresden.

Beyond that, specialized machinery for the automation sector is produced in Dresden by the company *XENON Automatisierungstechnik GmbH*. In the area of plant engineering, the organizations *Linde-KCA-Dresden* and *von Ardenne* are to be mentioned.

In the printing press domain, the *Koenig & Bauer AG*, with its registered office in Radebeul, is the technological leader for waterless offset printing presses.
As exemplary specialists for foodstuff- and packaging machines, the *Glatt Systemtechnik GmbH* and the *Theegarten-Pactec GmbH & Co. KG*, both with registered offices in Dresden, are to be mentioned. The economic sector is varied at the location and is able – across all political systems – to refer to a long operating experience.

International competition
In order for market opportunities to be recognized and utilized, innovations in products and processes to be offered and economic reserves be made available, the Free State of Saxony has founded the Verbundinitiative Maschinenbau Sachsen (VEMAS – Saxony mechanical enigineering network initiative). VEMAS consolidates specialized areas into organizational networks and technological projects. In this way, research and development can be promoted and innovative system solutions can be offered on the global market.
Since 2003, VEMAS has been operating on behalf of the Saxon State Ministry for Economic Affairs and Labour and it is administered by the Fraunhofer Institute for Machine Tools and Forming Technology (IWU). The initiative finds industrial support through the competence centre of the Maschinenbau Chemnitz/Sachsen eV (mechanical engineering association). The core tasks of the network initiative are the improvement of organizational innovation through technology transfer, the initiation of cooperation projects, supporting the development of new markets as well as the acquisition and assurance of highly qualified skilled personnel. For the development of innovation and efficiency of Saxon SMEs, the activities of VEMAS are aimed at sustainable collaboration between science and economy.
For this purpose, in 2009 VEMAS already for the second time organized a joint participation stand at the intec trade fair in Leipzig under the topic "Meeting Point for Industry and Science". The implementation of topic-specific workshops and the initiation and attendance of cooperation projects in this year lead to a further strengthening of the technological capacity of organizations.
The focus of the development of new markets is primarily aimed at Russia and India. In addition to the support of Saxon organizations in the target markets on location, the attendance of foreign delegations in Saxony also contributes towards the initiation of concrete cooperation projects.

Outlook
The global financial market crisis may afflict many economic sectors. Long-term success is however granted to those who focus on innovation. The research-intensive environment in the Dresden region is a guarantor of mechanical engineering in the region and the whole of Saxony for entrepreneurial success and therewith also for growth and employment in the long term. Investors are well-advised in and together with Saxony. Engineering – of course in Saxony!

Company Profile

Leybold Optics Dresden GmbH

Geschäftsführer/**Managers:**
Dr. Michael Liehr
Helmut Frankenberger

Gründungsjahr/**Year of foundation:**
2000

Mitarbeiter/**Employees:**
100

Umsatz/**Turnover:**
2007: 13,9 Millionen Euro/
2007: 13.9 million euros
2008: 25,9 Millionen Euro/
2008: 25.9 million euros

Geschäftstätigkeit/**Business activity:**
Sonderanlagenbau
Maschinenbau
Special systems engineering
Mechanical engineering

Anschrift/**Address:**
Zur Wetterwarte 50/Haus 303
D-01109 Dresden
Telefon +49 (0) 351 86695-16
Telefax +49 (0) 351 86695-17
info.dresden@leyboldoptics.com
www.leyboldoptics.com

Maßgeschneiderte Lösungen seit 150 Jahren
Taylored solutions for more than 150 years

Als bedeutendes Unternehmen der Vakuumtechnologie befasst sich Leybold Optics GmbH mit der Entwicklung und Herstellung von Anlagen zur Beschichtung von Oberflächen, vorwiegend von Glas und Kunststoffen. Das in Alzenau in Unterfranken beheimatete Unternehmen und sein Tochterunternehmen in Dresden gehören seit 2001 zur Investmentgruppe EQT und gelten als ein weltweit führender Hersteller von Vakuumsystemen.

Duch Innovation, Qualität sowie hochqualifizierte Mitarbeiter in den Bereichen Maschinenbau und Prozesstechnik setzt Leybold Optics technische Maßstäbe, die selbst die Wissenschaftler renommierter Fraunhofer-Institute regelmäßig auf das Know-how der Alzenauer und Dresdener Experten zurückgreifen lassen.

Der Traditionsname Leybold Optics steht dabei für modernste Beschichtungstechnologie und maßgeschneiderte Lösungen in den Bereichen 3D-Coating/Web, Display/Glass, Optics, Solar und Special Systems. Der Schwerpunkt liegt in Auslegung, Konstruktion und Bau von Vakuumprozess-Systemen, darüber hinaus in der Entwicklung und Implementierung von Vakuumprozessen für dünne Schichten, beispielsweise für die Herstellung photovoltaischer Zellen.

The field of excellence of Leybold Optics GmbH, a renowned vacuum systems manufacturer, is development and production of systems for the coating of surfaces, primarily those of glass and plastic substrates. The company headquarters located in Alzenau, a town in northern Bavaria, and its Dresden-based daughter company have been part of the Swedish private equity group EQT since 2001.

Highly innovative specialists in engineering and process technology are setting standards in technology and quality, which encourages even scientists of famous Fraunhofer Institutes to rely on the expertise of the Alzenau and Dresden experts.

The traditional name of Leybold Optics stands for state-of-the-art vacuum coating technology and tailored solutions in the fields of 3D-coating/web, display/glass, optics, solar und special systems. The company is focused on the design and manufacturing of vacuum process systems and the development and implementation of vacuum processes for the deposition of thin films, which may be used for the production of solar cells for example.

Oben:
Vertikale Vakuumbeschichtungsanlage A 1500 V-7.
Above: Vertical vacuum coating system A 1500 V-7.

Unten: Büro- und Produktionsgebäude von Leybold Optics Dresden.
Below: Office and production hall of Leybold Optics Dresden.

Company Profile

Die Zukunft fest im Griff – Der Spezialist für Bau- und Industriebedarf
The future well under control – The specialist for building and industrial materials

Die HTI Dinger & Hortmann KG ging aus der HTI „Mitteldeutschland" GmbH & Co. Handels KG hervor, die 1996 gegründet wurde. Ein Jahr später wurde die neu gebaute Niederlassung in Klipphausen bezogen. In den folgenden Jahren wurden Zug um Zug die heute bestehenden Niederlassungen und Abholstützpunkte in Betrieb genommen. Das Unternehmen ist damit flächendeckend in Sachsen sowie in Sachsen-Anhalt vertreten und mit seinen Logistikleistungen jederzeit schnell vor Ort.

HTI hat es sich zur Aufgabe gemacht, seinen Kunden ein zentraler Partner für das gesamte Sortiment rund um den Tiefbau- und Industriebedarf zu sein. Wo man früher noch mit verschiedenen Herstellern und Spezialhändlern zusammenarbeiten musste, bietet die HTI-Gruppe heute qualitativ hochwertige Systeme aus einer Hand. Das Portfolio umfasst zudem die Schwerpunkte: Versorgung und Entsorgung, Klärwerkstechnik, Regenwasserbewirtschaftung, Straßenbau, industrieller Rohrleitungsbau sowie Produkte für den Bereich regenerative Energien.

Mit einem hauseigenen Fuhrpark und gut ausgestatteten Lagern hat HTI – Die Zukunft fest im Griff.

The HTI Dinger & Hartmann KG is a successor company of the HTI "Mitteldeutschland" GmbH & Co. Handels KG, which was founded in 1996. One year later, the newly built branch in Klipphausen was settled into. In the following years, the currently existing branches were taken into operation step-by-step. Therewith the organization is extensively represented in Saxony as well as Saxony-Anhalt and with its logistics services is locally always readily available.

The HTI Dinger & Hartmann KG has made it their business to be a central partner for their clients for the entire range of products surrounding underground engineering and industrial materials. Where in the past it was necessary to co-operate with numerous producers and specialist traders, the HTI Group today offers premium quality systems from one source. In addition, the comprehensive portfolio encompasses the following focal points: utility supply and waste disposal, wastewater treatment plant technology, rainwater management, road construction, industrial pipeline construction as well as products for renewable energies.

With an in-house vehicle fleet and well-equipped warehouses HTI has – The future well under control.

HTI Dinger & Hortmann KG

Geschäftsführender Gesellschafter/Managing Partner: Thomas Dinger

Gründungsjahr/Year of foundation:
1996, hervorgegangen aus der HTI „Mitteldeutschland" GmbH & Co. Handels KG
A successor firm of HTI "Mitteldeutschland" GmbH & Co. Handels KG

Mitarbeiter/Employees:
über/more than 200
(43 Auszubildene/trainees)

Geschäftstätigkeit/Business activity:
Fachgroßhandel für Bau- und Industriebedarf; Verkauf von Produkten für die Bereiche Versorgung, Entsorgung, Klärwerkstechnik, Straßenbau, Regenwasserbewirtschaftung, Gebäudetechnik und regenerative Energien
Specialized wholesale trade for building and industrial materials; sale of products for the areas of utility supply, waste disposal, wastewater treatment plant technology, road construction, rainwater management, building services engineering and renewable energies

Anschrift/Address:
Postfach 120134
D-01002 Dresden
www.hti-dinger-hortmann.de

Niederlassungen/Branches:
Dresden-Klipphausen
Dresdner Straße 2
D-01665 Klipphausen
Telefon +49 (0) 35204 966-0
Telefax +49 (0) 35204 966-38

Torgau
Aueweg 1
D-04860 Torgau
Telefon +49 (0) 3421 7745-0
Telefax +49 (0) 3421 7745-16

Leipzig-Zwenkau
Baumeisterallee 37–39
D-04442 Zwenkau
Telefon +49 (0) 34203 568-0
Telefax+49 (0) 34203 568-99

Chemnitz-Röhrsdorf
Nordstraße 20
D-09247 Röhrsdorf
Telefon +49 (0) 3722 503-0
Telefax +49 (0) 3722 503-124

Magdeburg
Wörmlitzer Straße 6
D-39126 Magdeburg
Telefon +49 (0) 391 55543-0
Telefax+49 (0) 391 55543-30

Weitere Abholstützpunkte in/Further collection points in:
Leipzig-Engelsdorf, Halle/Saale, Zwickau, Halberstadt und Dresden

Mezzaninkapital – Innovative Finanzierungsmethoden für den Mittelstand
Mezzanine capital – Innovative financing methods for medium-sized businesses

Markus H. Michalow
Der Autor ist Gebietsleiter für das Personal, Private & Business Banking der Dresdner Bank AG in Dresden. Er hat eine Ausbildung zum Devisenhändler und im Bereich Kreditwesen bei der Deutschen Bank AG in Frankfurt absolviert und wirkte zuletzt in verschiedenen leitenden Funktionen bei der Deutschen Bank, den Dresdner Stadtwerken sowie der Dresdner Bank.
The author is the area manager for Personnel, Private & Business Banking at the Dresdner Bank AG in Dresden. He completed his training at the Deutsche Bank AG in Frankfurt as a forex dealer and in financing. He recently worked in various leadership positions at Deutsche Bank, Dresdner Stadtwerke (municipal utility company) as well as Dresdner Bank.

Die innovativste Finanzierungsmethode für mittelständische Unternehmen liegt im ganzheitlichen Beratungsansatz. Denn gerade bei inhabergeführten Unternehmen besteht eine enge Verbindung zwischen privaten und geschäftlichen Finanzen. Gemeinsam mit seinem Berater klärt der Kunde, welches Finanzierungsinstrument am besten zur eigenen Situation und den langfristigen geschäftlichen Zielen passt. Individuelle Wünsche und geschäftliche Ziele werden so aufeinander abgestimmt.

Neben dem Eigenkapital als vermögensbildender Substanz ist vor allem die private und geschäftliche Risikosituation des Unternehmens von zentraler Bedeutung. Die Interdependenzen, die hierbei auftreten können, begründen auch die Notwendigkeit eines ganzheitlichen Risikomanagements.

Unternehmensanalyse in zwei Schritten

Nachdem der erste Kontakt zu den kapitalsuchenden Unternehmen etabliert wurde, werden diese potenziellen Portfoliounternehmen in einem mehrstufigen Prozess mit den Kriterien des Kreditinstituts abgeglichen. Dadurch soll ein genauer Einblick in das Unternehmen bezüglich aller Stärken und Schwächen geschaffen werden, um so die Chancen und Risiken einer Beteiligung genauer erfassen zu können. Bevor die wirtschaftliche Lage des Unternehmens im Detail erfasst wird, kommt es zu einer Grobprüfung. Dabei werden die Markt- und Absatzchancen sowie die geschäftlichen Rahmenbedingungen für das Unternehmen analysiert. Die Grobprüfung ist als eine Art Vorprüfung zu sehen. Im Rahmen dieser Vorprüfung soll festgestellt werden, ob das Unternehmen grundsätzlich die Anforderungskriterien für eine mögliche Kreditvergabe erfüllt. Wesentlicher Bestandteil dieser Prüfung ist ein Businessplan, auf dessen Basis die Finanzierungsmöglichkeiten geprüft werden. Entscheidende Prüfmerkmale beziehen sich hierbei auf den Absatzmarkt des Unternehmens und auf das Management. Diese Grobprüfung erfordert ein in hohem Maß strukturiertes Vorgehen, um den Aufwand zu minimieren und keine Erfolg versprechenden Möglichkeiten zu übersehen.

In einer zweiten, detaillierteren Prüfung verschiebt sich der Schwerpunkt auf die gesellschaftsrelevanten, steuerrechtlichen und finanzierungstechnischen Fragen. Diese Prüfung verfolgt im Wesentlichen drei Hauptziele:
1. Offenlegung von Unternehmensinformationen
2. Analyse und Prüfung des Unternehmens

Financing

The most innovative financing methods for medium-sized enterprises lie in integrated consulting approaches. Especially in owner-managed enterprises, a close connection exists between private and business finances. Together with his consultant, the client decides which financial instrument best suites his position and long-term business goals. In this way individual needs and business objectives are coordinated.

In addition to equity capital as an asset creating substance, it is primarily the private and business risk position of the enterprise that is of key importance. The interdependencies that could occur in this connection also justify the necessity for an integrated risk management system.

Business analysis in two steps

Once the first contact has been established with the capital-seeking enterprise, the potential investment management company is matched to the criteria of the financial institution in a multi-stage process. In this way a precise insight is created into the enterprise as regards all its strengths and weaknesses in order to more accurately grasp the opportunities and risks of an investment. A rough assessment is first made prior to measuring the economic position in detail. In the process, the market opportunities and marketing potential as well as the general business conditions for the enterprise are analyzed. The rough assessment is to be seen as a type of preliminary examination. Within the scope of this preliminary examination it is to be determined whether the enterprise fundamentally fulfills the standard criteria for the possible granting of a loan. An essential part of this examination is a business plan, on the basis of which the financing possibilities are reviewed. Decisive inspection features here relate to the business market of the enterprise and its management. This rough assessment demands a highly structured approach in order to minimize costs and to avoid the oversight of promising success possibilities.

Kreditwesen

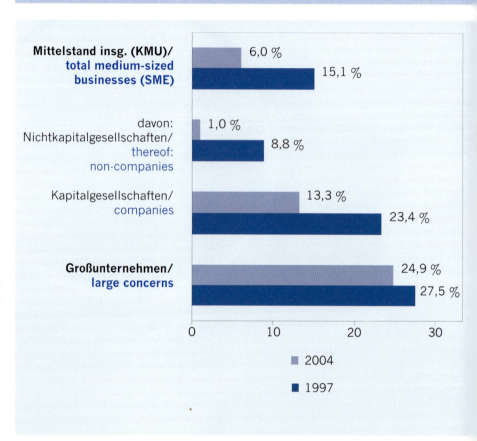

Bessere Konstitution des Mittelstands

Finanzielle Bestandsfestigkeit des Mittelstands bis 2004 klar erhöht. Eigenmittel in Prozent der Bilanzsumme.
The financial business persistence of medium-sized businesses clearly increased until 2004. Capital resources as a percentage of total assets.

Quelle/Source: Deutsche Bundesbank

3. Schaffung einer Entscheidungsgrundlage und Unterstützung der Preis-/Konditionsfindung

Eine integrierte Beratung soll nicht nur das Vermögen eines Unternehmens schützen und optimieren, sondern auch prüfen, ob das Unternehmen in der Eigenkapitalausstattung noch eine Lücke zu schließen hat. Gerade die mangelhafte Ausstattung mit Eigenkapital von Unternehmen stellt ein zentrales Problem vieler mittelständischer Unternehmen dar. Denn häufig ist der Eigenkapitalanteil der Unternehmen gering und der Anteil der Bankfinanzierung hoch. Zudem erodiert der Wert vieler Sicherheiten. Damit wird für diese Unternehmen die Frage der Außenfinanzierung mit Eigenkapital immer mehr zum zentralen Thema. Die Beschaffung von Eigenkapital durch die Emission von Anteilspapieren an der Börse ist jedoch nur Aktiengesellschaften vorbehalten. Dieser Weg der Eigenkapitalbeschaffung scheidet somit für die Mehrzahl kleiner und mittelständischer Unternehmen aus. Gerade aus diesem Grund sind alternative Finanzierungsmodelle gefragt.

Mezzaninfinanzierung

Da der deutsche Mittelstand für künftiges Wachstum mehr Risikofinanzierungen benötigt, setzen Banken mit neuen innovativen Konzepten an dieser Stelle an. Um die Eigenkapitalbasis von Unternehmen zu stärken, bieten Banken vermehrt standardisierte Mezzaninprodukte an, die auch kleineren Unternehmen den Weg zum Kapitalmarkt öffnen.

Mezzaninkapital bietet situationsspezifische, maßgeschneiderte, externe Finanzierungslösungen. Es lässt sich keiner der beiden idealtypischen Kategorien des *reinen Eigenkapitals* respektive des *reinen Fremdkapitals* eindeutig zuordnen. Für den Begriff der Mezzaninfinanzierung lässt sich weder in der Ökonomie noch in der Rechtswissenschaft eine eindeutige Definition ausmachen. Das Wort *Mezzanino* entstammt der Architektur und steht im Italienischen sinnbildlich für ein Zwischengeschoss zwischen Erd- und Obergeschoss. Wirtschaftlich gesehen handelt es sich bei diesem „Zwischengeschoss" um eine hybride Struktur zwischen Fremd- und Eigenkapital. Allerdings können diese hybriden Instrumente im Rahmen einer rechtlichen Betrachtung je nach Ausgestaltung eindeutig dem Eigen- oder Fremdkapital zugeordnet werden. Trotz seiner rechtlichen Einstufung in Eigen- oder Fremdkapital besteht die Besonderheit darin, dass es doch Eigenschaften der jeweils anderen Art besitzt. So kann diese hybride Finanzierungsform beispielsweise derart ausgestaltet werden, dass das investierte Kapital steuerliche Vorteile (zum Beispiel durch Abzugsfähigkeit der Zinsen) gewährleistet und außerdem gegenüber dem Eigenkapital vorrangig ist, aber trotzdem Eigenschaften von Eigenkapital aufweist.

Bei einer Mezzaninfinanzierung beteiligt sich der Kapitalgeber mit einem Nachrangdarlehen wirtschaftlich am Unternehmen

Financing

Better configuration of medium-sized businesses

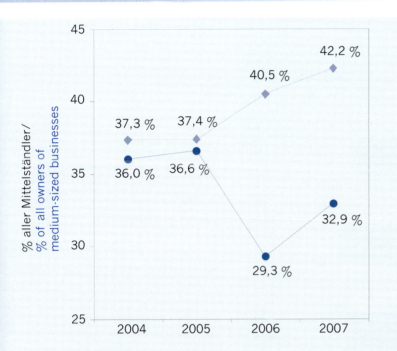

Auch nach 2004 weitere Verbesserung der Eigenkapitalausstattung im Mittelstand. Anteile in Prozent.
Also after 2004 further improvement of the equity capital configuration in the medium-sized sector. Percentage of shares.

Quelle/Source: Creditreform

In a second, more detailed examination, the focal point shifts to questions regarding societal topics, tax laws and finance. This examination primarily pursues three main objectives:
1. Disclosure of company information
2. Analysis and inspection of the company
3. Creation of a basis for decision-making and the support of pricing/condition determination

An integrated consultation should not only secure and optimize the assets of an organization, but rather also check whether there is a gap in the equity base of the organization that is to be bridged. Faulty equity facilities currently represent a central problem for many medium-sized enterprises. Frequently the own capital contribution is marginal and the portion financed by the bank high. In addition, the value of many securities is eroded. For this reason, the question of external financing through own capital becomes an ever more central issue for these organizations. The creation of equity capital through the issuance of shares on the stock exchange is however only reserved for companies. Consequently this eliminates the majority of smaller or medium-sized enterprises from creating equity capital in this way. It is precisely for this reason that alternative financing models are in demand.

Mezzanine financing

Since the German medium-sized enterprise sector requires more risk-financing for future growth, the banks at this point are ensuing new innovative concepts. In order to strengthen the equity capital base of organizations, banks are increasingly offering standardized mezzanine products, which also open the doorway to the capital market for smaller organizations.

Mezzanine capital offers external financing solutions which are tailor-made and situation-specific. It can not be assigned to one of the two ideal types of categories which are *eqiuity capital* and *external finance*. For the term mezzanine financing there is neither a clear definition represented in economics nor in law. The word *mezzanine* has its origin in architecture and in Italian, it symbolically stands for a floor between the ground and first floors. From an economic point of view, this "in between floor" is about a hybrid structure between external and equity capital. However, these hybrid instruments can, within the scope of legal consideration, clearly be assigned to equity or external capital respectively, according to design. Despite its legal grading into equity or external capital, the distinctive feature lies therein that each form still possesses characteristics of the other. In this way this hybrid financing form can for instance be developed in such a way that the invested capital ensures tax benefits (for example through the deductibility of the interest) and is furthermore preferential in comparison to equity capital, but nevertheless displays characteristics of equity capital.

Kreditwesen

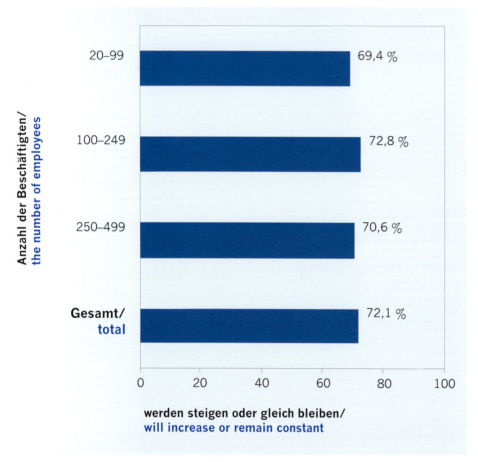

Investitionen 2008 weiter auf hohem Niveau
Angaben in Prozent der Befragten/
2008 investments continuing at a high level
data in percentage of respondents

Für 2008 erwartete Entwicklung der Investitionen in der Industrie nach Anzahl der Beschäftigten.
Industry investment developments expected for 2008 as per the number of employees.

Quelle/**Source**: BDI-Mittelstandspanel

Dabei kann es sich um ein reines Darlehen (Gesellschaftsdarlehen, partiarisches Darlehen), aber auch um eine Stellung als stiller Gesellschafter oder Genussrechtsinhaber handeln. Mezzaninkapital lässt sich also je nach Nähe der Konstruktion zu reinem Eigen- oder Fremdkapital in *Equity Mezzanine* und *Debt Mezzanine* unterscheiden.

Vom Risiko her nimmt die Mezzaninfinanzierung eine Mittelstellung zwischen dem klassischen Darlehen gegen Sicherheiten und dem Eigenkapital ein. Charakteristika dieses Finanzierungskonzepts sind Nachrangigkeit, steuerliche Abzugsfähigkeit, Kündbarkeit, Flexibilität, ein breiter Anlegerkreis und vielseitige Anwendungsmöglichkeiten. Bei der Bereitstellung von Mezzaninfinanzierungen ist für den Kapitalgeber nicht allein die Bonität des Unternehmens entscheidend: Er orientiert sich zumeist an den erwarteten Cashflows oder an Verpflichtungserklärungen des Kapitalnehmers, mittels derer bestimmte Informations-, Mitwirkungs- oder Kontrollrechte eingeräumt werden. In der Regel erfolgt die Tilgung erst nach sieben bis zwölf Jahren, was eine – im Vergleich zu sechs bis neun Jahren bei sonstigen Bankkrediten – recht lange Laufzeit bedeutet.

Für sein Darlehen erhält der Nachrangkapitalgeber mangels Sicherheiten eine um mindestens zwei Prozentpunkte höhere Verzinsung als der herkömmliche Darlehensgeber. Mezzaninfinanzierungen bieten sich an, wenn haftendes Eigenkapital nicht hinreichend beschafft werden kann und herkömmliche, kommerzielle Kredite aufgrund mangelnder Sicherheiten nicht oder nur begrenzt gewährt werden.

Mezzaninkapital gewinnt an Bedeutung

Darüber hinaus kann eine solche Finanzierung, bei richtiger Strukturierung, durch die Zurechnung des Mezzaninkapitals zum Eigenkapital des Unternehmens zu einer entsprechenden Verbesserung des Ratings bei der Bank führen. Es ist davon auszugehen, dass solch innovative Finanzierungsmethoden in den nächsten Jahren an Bedeutung gewinnen werden. Dieses steigende Angebot wird schließlich Druck auf die aktuellen Konditionen ausüben. Darum dürften aus Sicht der mittelständischen Unternehmen kapitalmarktnahe Finanzierungen in den nächsten Jahren tendenziell günstiger werden, was das erwartete Ansteigen des allgemeinen Zinsniveaus teilweise kompensieren könnte. Eines ist damit klar: Alternative Finanzierungsmethoden werden auch in Zukunft deutlich attraktiver.

Financing

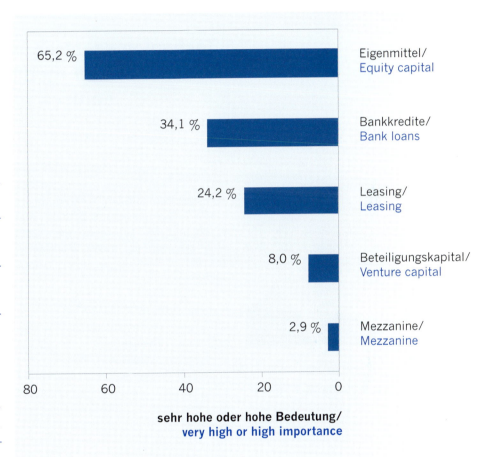

Investitionen 2008 weiter auf hohem Niveau
Angaben in Prozent der Befragten/
**2008 investments continuing at a high level
data in percentage of respondents**

Bedeutung von Finanzierungsbausteinen für die 2008 geplanten Investitionen.
Importance of financing building blocks for investments planned for 2008.

- 65,2 % — Eigenmittel/ Equity capital
- 34,1 % — Bankkredite/ Bank loans
- 24,2 % — Leasing/ Leasing
- 8,0 % — Beteiligungskapital/ Venture capital
- 2,9 % — Mezzanine/ Mezzanine

sehr hohe oder hohe Bedeutung/
very high or high importance

In mezzanine financing, the financier with a subordinate loan participates commercially in the organization. Thereby this can only be a pure loan or the financier holds the position of a silent partner or a profit participation proprietor. Thus, depending on the proximity of the structure to pure equity or pure external capital, mezzanine capital distinguishes itself in *equity mezzanine* and *debt mezzanine*.

From a risk point of view, mezzanine financing takes a mid-position between the classical loan issued against security and equity capital. The characteristics of this financing concept are subordination, tax deductibility, redeemability, flexibility, a broad range of investors and versatile application possibilities. The creditworthiness of the organization alone is not decisive for the financier in the provision of mezzanine financing: He mostly orientates himself to the expected cash flow or a commitment from the capital seeker, by means of his acknowledgement of specific rights to information, cooperation and control. As a rule, repayment only occurs after seven to twelve years, which, in comparison with six to nine years with other bank loans, means a really long timespan.

In the absence of security for his loan, the subordinate financier obtains an interest rate at least two per cent higher than the conventional loan financier. Mezzanine financing offers itself when liable equity cannot sufficiently be obtained and conventional, commercial loans are not or only restrictedly allowed due to a lack of security.

Mezzanine capital gains in importance

Furthermore, any such financing, with the correct structuring, through the addition of mezzanine capital to the equity capital of the organization, could lead to a corresponding improvement of rating at the bank. It is to be assumed that such innovative financing methods will gain in importance within the next few years. This upstream proposition will ultimately exert pressure on the current conditions. From the perspective of medium-sized enterprises, capital market friendly financing methods are likely to become cheaper within the next few years, which could partially compensate for the expected increase in the general interest level. Therewith one thing is evident: Alternative financing methods will also in future become notably more attractive.

Tradition und Moderne – Technologiezentren im Innovationswettbewerb
Traditional and modern spirits – Technology centres in innovative competition

Dr. Wilhelm W. Zörgiebel
Der Autor wurde 1953 geboren und hat nach dem Abitur in Darmstadt Wirtschaftsingenieurwesen studiert. Es folgten ein Studienaufenthalt an der Harvard Business School in Boston und 1983 die Promotion. Nach der Wiedervereinigung wirkte er als Unternehmensberater. Seit 1998 ist er Geschäftsführer der Grundbesitz Hellerau GmbH und an verschiedenen Biotechnologieunternehmen beteiligt.
The author was born in 1953 and after completing his A-levels, studied engineering and management in Darmstadt. This was followed by a study stay at the Harvard Business School in Boston and the conferral of a doctorate in 1983. After German reunification he worked as a management consultant. Since 1998 he has been the managing director of the Grundbesitz Hellerau GmbH and has also been involved in numerous biotechnology organizations.

Anziehungskraft schöpft Dresden heute aus vielschichtigen Verknüpfungen von Kultur, Industrie und Bildung. Wirtschaft und Wissenschaft der Stadt profitieren von lebendigen Traditionen, die weit in die Vergangenheit zurückreichen.

Für die weitere Entwicklung ist entscheidend, kreative Potenziale – Menschen und Institutionen – so gut mit einander ins Gespräch zu bringen, dass dauerhaft Neues entsteht: Ideen, Forschungsfragen, Wissen, Produkte und Kooperationen – Innovationen. Einen Widerhall findet dieses Neue dann nicht nur in der Welt der Wirtschaft und in Wettbewerbsvorteilen, sondern in Forschung und Lehre, Kunst und Kultur, denn Innovationen erschöpfen sich nicht allein in Technologien und Markterfolg.

Eine wesentliche Rolle spielen dabei Technologie- und Gründerzentren als Orte, an denen Wissen und Kommunikation einen produktiven Nährboden finden. Was zeichnet diese Orte aus? Welche besonderen Eigenschaften muss eine Immobilie – ein Gebäude oder ein Standort – bieten, um attraktiv zu sein für wissensintensive Unternehmen und ihre Mitarbeiter? Wie können eine Immobilie und ihr Management für sie Mehrwert schaffen?

Vor einhundert Jahren wurde Hellerau am Rande Dresdens erbaut, gründend auf dem Gartenstadt-Gedanken, um Arbeit, Wohnen, Bildung und Natur zu vereinen. Heute, mit dem Wachsen der Wissensgesellschaft, siedeln dort Unternehmen der Hochtechnologie. Am Beispiel des GebäudeEnsembles Deutsche Werkstätten Hellerau wird deutlich: Vermietung, Gastronomie und Veranstaltungsmanagement in einem technologieorientierten Umfeld funktionieren nicht als Immobilienverwaltung im klassischen Sinne. Warum? Erfolgreiche Ideen, Geschäftsmodelle und Unternehmen wachsen zuerst in den Köpfen von Menschen. Kraft gewinnen sie dann im Austausch mit anderen und geduldige Arbeit an „echten" lebendigen Orten.

Zwar liegen die Vorteile der Digitalisierung auf der Hand: Entfernungen schrumpfen. Menschen rücken zusammen. Geschäfte werden schneller. Kosten sinken. Dienstreisen sind heute längst nicht das einzige Mittel, gemeinsam mit anderen an Projekten zu arbeiten und sich auf dem Laufenden zu halten. Aber ein guter Unternehmensstandort ist mehr ein dichtes Dach über einem kreativen Kopf, mit schneller Internetverbindung und Hausmeisterservice.

Today Dresden creates attraction from a multilayered connection of culture, industry and education. The economy and science of the city profit from living traditions which go back far into the past.

For further development, it is decisive to get creative potentials – people and institutions – to communicate so well with each other that new ideas are continually created: ideas, research issues, knowledge, products and co-operation – innovations. These new ideas will then not only be echoed in the scientific world and in competitive advantages, but also in research and education, art and culture, because innovations are not only restricted to technologies and market success.

Thereby, technology and foundation centres play a significant role as places in which knowledge and communication find a productive breeding ground. What distinguishes these locations? Which special characteristics should real estate – a building or a location – offer in order to be attractive for knowledge-intensive organizations and their employees? How can real estate and its management create added value for them?

A hundred years ago, Hellerau was built on the edge of Dresden, founded on the garden cities concept to unite working, living, education and nature. Today, with the growth of the knowledge economy, high-tech organisations settle there. Using the example of GebäudeEnsemble Deutsche Werkstätten Hellerau, it becomes clear: Letting, gastronomy and event management in a technology-oriented environment do not function as real estate management in the classical sense.

Ein unternehmerisch geführtes Technologiezentrum als Adresse für technologieorientierte Unternehmen und Existenzgründer muss deshalb auf Prinzipien aufbauen, die im Folgenden zusammengefasst sind.

Nachhaltig bauen

Ein Gebäude, das – für den Möbelbau vor 100 Jahren visionär geplant und erbaut – noch heute zweckmäßige moderne Arbeitsbedingungen für Labore, Büros und Gewerbe bietet, darf verdientermaßen als wert- und nachhaltig bezeichnet werden. Dies ist der Anspruch an nachhaltige Architektur, in der Wissen und Kommunikation als Antriebskräfte wirken. Der Mensch mit seiner Handwerkskunst und Kreativität ist das Maß für die Gestaltung seiner Umgebung.

Vielfalt gewinnt

Vielfalt ist eine Ressource. Impulse für Neues entstehen dann, wenn sich Menschen und Themen begegnen, die bisher wenig miteinander zu tun hatten, zum Beispiel Forscher und Unternehmer und Künstler. Zündende Ideen brauchen Konfrontation, um zu reifen. Und zugleich verspricht ein guter Mietermix Schutz vor Konjunkturschwankungen.

Kommunikation und kurze Wege

Offene Kommunikation in alle Richtungen schafft Gelegenheiten für Kooperationen. Technologie- und Gründerzentren sind nur erfolgreich, wenn sie stetig dafür sorgen, dass ihre Mieter und deren Partner nicht allein bleiben. Sie haben somit eine Plattformfunktion. Die Forschungs- und Unternehmenslandschaft in Dresden bietet dafür vielfältige Kontakte und Netzwerke. Ist die unmittelbare Nähe zur Technischen Universität Dresden und zu den Forschungsinstituten deshalb für Gründer und wachsende Unternehmen ein unverzichtbarer Standortfaktor? Ich denke nicht, denn Dresden ist vor allem eine Stadt der kurzen Wege. Forschungsinstitute und Technologieparks finden sich in allen Teilen der Stadt. Entscheidend ist doch, wie gut diese Verbindungen tragen und wie es jungen Unternehmen gelingt, schnell Kontakte zu finden und Netzwerke zu knüpfen, die eine Geschäftsidee zum Erfolg führen.

Markenpflege

Wem es gelingt, einen Ort als lebendige Marke zu etablieren, wird Mieter finden und binden, die ihrerseits zugleich die Attraktivität des Standorts verstärken. Für junge Unternehmen bieten Technologiezentren in erster Linie ein Versprechen auf Geschäftserfolg in einem innovationsgetriebenen Umfeld.

Wachstum und Wandel

Junge und erfolgreiche Unternehmen wachsen oder sie gründen Tochterfirmen. In der Fähigkeit, immer wieder neue Freiräume für Nutzer zu schaffen, die sich kontinuierlich verändern, liegt die unternehmerische Herausforderung für private Technologie- und Gründerzentren.

Start-up

Why? Successful ideas, business models and organizations first grow in the minds of people. They only obtain strength in exchange with others and patient work at "real" lively locations.

Although the advantages of digitalization are obvious: Distances are shrinking. People are moving together. Business is becoming faster. Costs are sinking. Today, business trips are by far not the only means to work with other people on projects and to keep updated. However, a good business location is more than a thick roof over a creative head with fast internet connections and caretaker service.

A entrepreneurial managed technology centre as a location for technology-oriented organizations and entrepreneurs must therefore be based on principles which have been summarized below.

Sustainable building

A building, which – planned and built with vision 100 years ago for furniture construction – today still offers functional modern working conditions for laboratories, offices and industry, may deservedly be labelled as recoverable and sustainable. This is the requirement of sustainable architecture, where knowledge and communication are the driving forces. With his handicraft and creativity, a person sets the standard for the design of his environment.

Diversity wins

Diversity is a resource. Impulses for new ideas originate when people and topics meet which up to now have had little to do with each other, for example researchers and businessmen and artists. Brilliant ideas need confrontation to mature. And simultaneously, a good mix of tenants assures protection against economic fluctuations.

Communication and short distances

Open communication in all directions creates opportunities for cooperation, and technology and foundation centres are only successful when they consistently ensure that their tenants and partners are not alone.

Erfolgreiche Ideen, Geschäftsmodelle und Unternehmen wachsen zuerst in den Köpfen von Menschen.
Successful ideas, business models and organizations first grow in the minds of people.

Internationaler Wettbewerb und Kooperation

Dresden ist der Wachstumsmotor der Region. Und zugleich gilt: Die Weltwirtschaft ist überall. Zum Glück, wie ich finde! Weltoffenheit ist deshalb der richtige Weg, die Anziehungskraft der Region zu verstärken. Inspiration entsteht doch zumeist im Kontakt mit vermeintlich Fremden im gewohnten Umfeld.

Betont werden muss: Diese Prinzipien sind kein Patentrezept, eher Elemente für den Erfolg eines wissens- und technologieorientierten Gewerbestandorts. Orte wie das GebäudeEnsemble Deutsche Werkstätten Hellerau, die aus sich heraus ein Geheimnis verraten, ohne alles preiszugeben, geraten nicht in Vergessenheit. Wirtschaft und Wissenschaft verstärken sich im besten Fall gegenseitig und zugleich andere Bereiche der Gesellschaft. Das ist die große Stärke, die Dresden und Hellerau als Lebens- und Arbeitsort so attraktiv macht.

They have a platform function. For this, the research and organisation landscape in Dresden offers manifold contacts and networks. Is the close proximity to the Dresden University of Technology and to the research institutions therefore an indispensable location factor for founders and growing organizations?

I do not think not, as Dresden is above all a city of short distances. Research institutions and technology parks are found in all parts of the city. Decisive is however, how well these connections bear up and how successful young organizations are in finding contacts and establishing networks fast, which leads a business idea towards success.

Brand management
Who ever manages to establish a location as a living brand, will find and bind tenants, who for their part simultaneously strengthen the attractiveness of the location. In the first place, technology centres offer young organizations an assurance for business success in an innovation-driven environment.

Growth and change
Young and successful organizations grow or they found subsidiaries. The ability to constantly create new spaces for occupants who are continuously changing is an entrepreneurial challenge for private technology and foundation centres.

International
competition and cooperation
Dresden is the growth motor for the region. And simultaneously essential is: The world economy is everywhere. Luckily, I think! Cosmopolitanism is therefore the right way to strengthen the attractiveness of the region. Inspiration, however, mostly originates through contact with supposed strangers in familiar surroundings.

It must be emphasized: These principles are no patent recipes, but rather elements for success for a knowledge and technology-oriented business location. Places such as Gebäude-Ensemble Deutsche Werkstätten Hellerau, which spontaneously reveal a secret without divulging everything, are not forgotten.

Economics and science at best mutually strengthen each other and other areas of society at the same time. That is the great strength which makes Dresden and Hellerau as a living and working location so attractive.

Company Profile

Grundbesitz Hellerau GmbH

Geschäftsführer/Managing Directors:
Dr. Wilhelm Zörgiebel
Dr. Wolfgang Thiele

Gründungsjahr/Year of foundation:
1998

Mitarbeiter/Employees:
8

Geschäftstätigkeit/Business activity:
Vermietung, Technologietransfer,
Tagungen, Kongresse, Immobilien,
Kunst, Gastronomie
Letting, technology transfer,
conferences, congresses, real estate,
art, gastronomy

Anschrift/Address:
Moritzburger Weg 67
D-01109 Dresden
Telefon +49 (0) 351 8838-201
Telefax +49 (0) 351 8838-245
info@hellerau-gb.de
www.hellerau-gb.de

GebäudeEnsemble Deutsche Werkstätten Hellerau – Ort für junge Unternehmen
GebäudeEnsemble Deutsche Werkstätten Hellerau – Location for new businesses

Das GebäudeEnsemble Deutsche Werkstätten Hellerau ist ein erstklassiger Standort für wissensintensive Unternehmen in Dresden. In den Räumen, in denen seit 1909 die Handwerker der renommierten Deutschen Werkstätten Hellerau hochwertige Inneneinrichtungen schufen, arbeiten heute Biotech-Unternehmen, Energieanlagenbauer, Softwareentwickler, selbständige Kreative und Künstler.

Der Grundbesitz Hellerau GmbH gelang es, seit 2000 das gesamte Areal als internationalen Gewerbestandort neu auszurichten und denkmalgerecht zu sanieren. Zudem ist das GebäudeEnsemble Deutsche Werkstätten Hellerau heute als Tagungs- und Veranstaltungsort im Dresdner Norden etabliert.

Die repräsentativen und traditionsbewusst gestalteten Räume werden für Kongresse, Seminare, Produktpräsentationen, Galas und für private Feierlichkeiten genutzt. Im 2.500 Quadratmeter großen Innenhof finden alljährlich Sommerfeste und andere Open-Air-Events statt. Ein Feinschmeckerrestaurant bietet vor Ort ungewöhnliche, kreative Küche und Genuss.

Die Verbindung von Arbeit, Wohnen, Natur, Bildung und Kunst prägt die Anziehungskraft des GebäudeEnsemble Deutsche Werkstätten Hellerau.

The GebäudeEnsemble Deutsche Werkstätten Hellerau is a first-class location for skill-intensive businesses in Dresden. In its rooms craftsmen of the renowned Deutsche Werkstätten Hellerau have been producing high-quality interior furnishing since 1909, while today they are the common working place of biotech enterprises, energy plant manufacturers, software developers, creative freelancers and artists.

The real estate company Grundbesitz Hellerau GmbH succeeded in renovating the entire area according to historical monument regulations and reorganizing it as an international business location. In addition, the GebäudeEnsemble Hellerau has become an established conference and event location in the north of Dresden.

The interior, embellished prestigiously and tradition-consciously, are a venue for congresses, seminars, product presentations, galas and for private celebrations. Annual summer festivals and other open-air events take place in the 2,500-square-meter inner yard. A gourmet restaurant offers extraordinary, creative cuisine.

The GebäudeEnsemble Deutsche Werkstätten Hellerau combine unit work, living, nature, education and art to a melange of exceptional attraction.

Company Profile

Schiffsbau mit Tradition –
Bestes Know-how aus Dresden
Shipbuilding with tradition –
Best know-how from Dresden

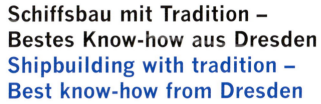

Schiffs- und Yachtwerft Dresden GmbH

Geschäftsführer/Manager:
Dipl.-Ing. Torsten Müller

Gründungsjahr/Year of foundation:
1898 in Dresden Laubegast;
2005 Übernahme
1898 in Laubegast, Dresden;
Buy-out in 2005

Mitarbeiter/Employees: 26

Geschäftstätigkeit/Business activity:
Schiffbau, Schiffsneubau,
Schiffsreparaturen, Stahlbau,
Stahlschiffbau, Holzschiffbau,
Edelstahl/Aluminium, Maschinenbau,
Motoreninstandsetzung, Schiffselektrik,
Innenausbau, Schiffssektionen, Aufbauten,
Binnenschifffahrt, Fahrgastschiffe, Fähren,
Schwimmende und feste Bauwerke
und Konstruktionen,
Entwurf und Konstruktion
Shipbuilding, new ship construction,
ship repairs, steel building,
steel ship building, wooden ship building,
stainless steel/aluminium,
mechanical engineering,
engine overhauling, ship electronics,
interior fittings, ship sections, superstructure,
inland navigation, passenger ships, ferries,
floating and fixed structures and constructions,
design and construction

Anschrift/Address:
Österreicher Straße 95
D-01279 Dresden
Telefon +49 (0) 351 2111170
Telefax +49 (0) 351 2111199
info@sywdresden.de
www.sywdresden.de

Aushängeschild der Werft:
die Rekonstruktion historischer Seitenraddampfer.
Shipyard signboard: the reconstruction
of historical side-paddle steamships.

Personendampfer „Krippen", Baujahr 1892.
The steam-powered passenger ship "Krippen",
year of construction 1892.

Refit, Rennboot BMW Veritas, Baujahr 1950.
Refitting of the BMW Veritas racing boat,
year of construction 1950.

Bereits seit über hundert Jahren werden in der Schiffs- und Yachtwerft Dresden GmbH Schiffe repariert, umgebaut und neu hergestellt. Ein besonderer Schwerpunkt der Werft liegt in der Anwendung historischer Techniken, wie der Niettechnik, sowie in der Reparatur von Dampfmaschinen. So konnten hier beispielsweise die über hundert Jahre alten Seitenraddampfer rekonstruiert werden. Über lange Zeit prägten diese Dampfer das Stadtbild Dresdens neben Frauenkirche, Semperoper und Zwinger. Dank der Werft gehören sie heute zu den bedeutenden touristischen Attraktionen der Stadt. Aber auch moderne innovative Schiffstechnik wird von der Schiffs- und Yachtwerft Dresden entwickelt und angeboten. Im Bereich Refit werden wertvolle Rennboote und Motoryachten saniert. Eine werfteigene Designabteilung widmet sich zudem dem Bereich mobiles Wohnen und dem Leben auf dem Wasser. Über die Slipanlage der Werft können Schiffe mit einer Länge von bis zu 80 Metern auf Land aufgenommen und auch zu Wasser gelassen werden. Aufgrund des Standorts an der Elbe ist die Werft von allen europäischen Schifffahrtsgebieten aus erreichbar. Mit ihrem vielfältigen Angebot leistet die Schiffs- und Yachtwerft Dresden einen bedeutenden Beitrag zur Binnenschifffahrt der Region Dresden.

For already more than one hundred years ships have been repaired, reconstructed and newly manufactured at the Schiffs- und Yachtwerft Dresden GmbH. A particular focal point of the shipyard lies in the application of historical technologies such as rivet technology, as well as in the repair of steam engines. That way for instance, the more than one hundred-year-old side-paddle steam engines could be reconstructed. For a long time this steam engines moulded the cityscape of Dresden, alongside the Frauenkirche (Church of Our Lady), the Semper Opera House and the Zwinger Palace. Thanks to the shipyard, they today belong to the most distinguished tourist attractions in the city. However, modern innovative shipping technology is also offered and developed at the Schiffs- und Yachtwerft Dresden. In the area of refitting, valuable racing boats and motor yachts are renovated. Moreover, at the shipyard's own design department, the ambit of mobile living and life on water is addressed. Via the shipyard's patent-slip dock site, ships with a length of up to 80 metres can be taken on land and also be set to water. Due to its location on the Elbe river, the shipyard is also accessible from all European navigation areas. With its wide variety of offers, the Schiffs- und Yachtwerft Dresden makes a considerable contribution to inland navigation of the Dresden region.

Dresden erlangt Topposition in der Kongress- und Tagungsbranche
Dresden gained top position in the congress and conference business

Gerhard Riegger

Der Autor wurde 1954 geboren und absolvierte eine Lehre zum Hotelkaufmann, die er 1971 abschloss. Es folgten die in der internationalen Hotellerie üblichen Lehrjahre in London, Frankreich und Rom. 1994 eröffnete er als Direktor das Hotel Albrechtshof Berlin. Seit 1997 ist er als Direktor für die MARITIM Hotelgesellschaft tätig, zuerst in Berlin und Halle und seit 2003 in Dresden.

The author was born in 1954 and completed an apprenticeship in hotel management in 1971. He subsequently completed a few years of apprenticeships, which are common practice in the hotel industry – in London, France and Rome. In 1994 he opened the Albrechtshof hotel in Berlin as director. He has been a director of the MARITIM Hotel Group since 1997, first in Berlin and Halle and since 2003, in Dresden.

Dresden, Landeshauptstadt Sachsens mit rund 510.000 Einwohnern: unzählig die Schätze in den Museen, atemberaubend die Schönheit der Architektur, erstaunlich die Vielfalt und das Niveau des traditionsreichen Musiklebens und überraschend die romantische Landschaft, die entlang der Elbe bis in die Innenstadt reicht.

Doch besitzt Dresden nicht nur als Kunst- und Kulturstadt einen hervorragenden Ruf. Die sächsische Landeshauptstadt gehört außerdem zu den Top 10 der deutschen Tagungs- und Kongressstädte. Die kontinuierliche Weiterentwicklung als Veranstaltungsdestination wurde unter anderem auch mit der Verleihung des Conga-Awards 2007 der Vereinigung Deutscher Veranstaltungsorganisatoren eV gewürdigt.

232 Konferenzen ab 250 Teilnehmern fanden 2007 in Dresden statt und untermauern die hohe Attraktivität der Stadt. 83 Prozent der Tagungsteilnehmer kamen aus Deutschland, 17 Prozent aus dem Ausland. Moderne Tagungshäuser und außergewöhnliche Veranstaltungsstätten zentral in der Stadt oder in Dresdens attraktiver Umgebung bieten sowohl Platz für kleine Meetings als auch große Konferenzen.

Direkt am Elbufer, fußläufig zum historischen Altstadtkern von Dresden, bietet das MARITIM Hotel & Internationale Congress Center Dresden seit 2006 beziehungsweise 2004 einen einzigartigen Rahmen für Meetings, Kongresse, Präsentationen und Festlichkeiten.

Das Internationale Congress Center Dresden (ICD) gilt seit seiner Eröffnung als eines der modernsten und erfolgreichsten Kongresshäuser Deutschlands. Mit seinen 35 Sälen und Räumen mit Platz für bis zu 6.500 Personen, seinen multifunktionalen Einrichtungen, der hochmodernen Tagungstechnik und dem umfangreichen Serviceangebot eignet es sich perfekt für Tagungs- und Kongressveranstaltungen aller Art. Seine einzigartige Lage direkt am grünen Elbufer und inmitten des historischen Altstadtkerns macht es besonders interessant. Aber auch die ungewöhnliche Architektur des Kongresszentrums inspiriert: Der zur Elbe hin wellenförmige, transparente Bau erlaubt einen weiten Blick auf die Dresdner Stadtsilhouette. Seit nunmehr über vier Jahren ist das ICD erfolgreich im nationalen und internationalen Kongressmarkt etabliert. In dieser Zeit fanden hier mehr als 2.238 Veranstaltungen mit circa 961.700 Teilnehmern aus 120 verschiedenen Ländern statt. Kongresse wie zum Beispiel die 120. IATA Flugplankonferenz, der „World Congress of Huntington's Disease" oder die „International Supercomputing Conference" belegen, dass der Standort Dresden im weltweiten Vergleich ohne Probleme mithalten kann und es nicht an der Vielfalt von Fachbereichen mangelt.

Congress Location

Am Puls der Zeit – Das Internationale Congress Center Dresden zählt zu den modernsten und schönsten Einrichtungen seiner Art.
With the times – The International Congress Center Dresden ranks among the most modern and beautiful establishments of its kind.

Dresden, the state capital of Saxony, with around 510,000 inhabitants: Innumerable are the treasures in the museums, breathtaking the beauty of the architecture, astonishing the diversity and the standard of the musical life, which is rich in tradition, and surprising the romantic landscape, which alongside the Elbe river reaches right into the city centre.

However, Dresden not only enjoys an outstanding reputation as an arts and culture city. The Saxon state capital in addition belongs to the top ten German conference and congress cities. The continuous advancement as an event destination was, amongst other things, also recognized with the Conga Award 2007 of the Vereinigung Deutscher Veranstaltungsorganisatoren eV (an association of German event organizers).

232 conferences with a minimum of 250 participants took place in Dresden in 2007 and confirm the high level of attractiveness of the city. 83 per cent of the congress participants came from Germany, 17 per cent from abroad. Modern conference buildings and superb event facilities in the city centre or in Dresden's beautiful surrounding area offer enough room for small meetings as well as large conferences.

Directly on the banks of the Elbe river, within walking distance of the historical city centre of Dresden, the MARITIM Hotel & International Congress Center Dresden has offered a unique setting for meetings, congresses, presentations and festivities since 2006, or 2004, respectively.

Seit der Eröffnung des ICD hat sich das internationale Gästevolumen in Dresden stetig gesteigert. Dieser Trend wird sich auch in den nächsten Jahren noch weiter fortsetzen. Eine wesentliche Grundlage dafür ist die gute Fluganbindung der Stadt an die wichtigsten internationalen Drehkreuze Frankfurt am Main und München. Derzeit zählt Frankfurt 47 und München 46 Starts pro Woche. Von dort bestehen zahlreiche internationale Verbindungen, die bislang von Dresden aus nicht angeflogen werden. Insgesamt gibt es vom Dresdner Flughafen aus 44 nationale und internationale Direktflüge. Auch die internationalen Flughäfen Prag und der neue Berliner Flughafen BBI sind mit 1,5 Stunden Fahrtzeit schnell zu erreichen und stehen positiv für die internationale Anbindung Dresdens. Auch wird das Streckennetz der Deutschen Bahn weiter ausgebaut. Dies sind Faktoren, die Dresden zu einer Topposition in der Kongressbranche verhelfen. Auch die sehr kurzen Wege in der Stadt tragen dazu bei. So kann man innerhalb des Altstadtkerns alles in nur wenigen Minuten zu Fuß erreichen und ist nicht auf Transferleistungen angewiesen.

Darüber hinaus besticht die Stadt mit ihrer hohen Zahl an weltbekannten Kunstschätzen und Sehenswürdigkeiten sowie mit ihrer lebendigen Kulturszene.

Das futuristische Gebäude liegt in unmittelbarer Nähe zur Semperoper und zu den Brühlschen Terrassen.
The futuristic buildings lie in the immediate vicinity of the Semper Opera and the Brühlsche Terrassen (a 500-metre-long "balcony").

Congress Location

Since its opening, the International Congress Center Dresden (ICD) has been deemed to be one of the most modern and successful congress centres in Germany. Its 35 halls and rooms, which house up to 6,500 people, its multifunctional facilities, ultra modern conference technology and the comprehensive range of services make it perfectly suitable for all kinds of conference and congress events. Its unique location directly on the green banks of the Elbe river and amidst the historical city centre makes it particularly interesting. The unusual architecture of the congress centre also inspires one: The wavelike, transparent building facing the Elbe river allows for a wide view over Dresden's skyline. For more than four years now, the ICD has been successfully established in the national and international congress market. During this period, more than 2,238 events with about 961,700 participants from 120 different countries have taken place. Congresses such as the 120th IATA Flight Plan Conference, the World Congress of Huntington's Disease or the International Supercomputing Conference vouch for the fact that the Dresden location can hold its own in worldwide comparison without problems, and that it does not have a shortage of diversity in speciality areas.

Since the opening of the ICD, international guest volumes in Dresden have steadily been increasing. This trend will also still continue further over the coming years. A significant foundation therefore is the city's good flight connection to the most important international hubs – Frankfurt am Main and Munich. Currently, Frankfurt totals 47 and Munich 46 take-offs per week. From there, numerous international connections are possible that have not headed out of Dresden until now. In total, there are 44 national and international direct flights from Dresden Airport. Also the distance to Prague International Airport and the new Berlin Airport (BBI) is easily reached in 1.5 hours of travelling time, which is favourabe for Dresden's international connection. Even the railway network of the Deutsche Bahn (German Rail) is being enlarged. These are factors which help Dresden to be at a top position in the congress sector. The short distances in the city also contribute to this. Thus, one can reach everything within the historical city centre by foot in a few minutes and without being dependant on transport services.

Furthermore, the city distinguishes itself with its great number of art treasures and places of interest, as well as with its lively cultural scene.

Kongressstandort

Die Region Dresden ist die bedeutendste Wachstumsregion im Osten Deutschlands. Sie ist auf dem Weg, sich zu einem der wichtigsten Wirtschafts- und Wissenschaftsstandorte in Deutschland zu entwickeln. So ist Dresden bei verschiedenen Wirtschaftsrankings (Prognos Zukunftsatlas, Bellevue Städtetest, Capital-Städterankings) immer auf einer der vorderen Positionen zu finden. Die Wirtschaft der Stadt stützt sich auf ein breites Branchenspektrum. Die entscheidenden Wachstums- und Entwicklungsimpulse gehen dabei von drei zukunftsorientierten Kompetenzfeldern aus: Mikroelektronik/Informations- und Kommunikationstechnologie, Nanotechnologie/Neue Werkstoffe und Life Sciences/Biotechnologie. Durch den stetigen Aus- und Aufbau dieser neuen Branchen besteht zusätzlich eine hohe Dichte an Forschungseinrichtungen (Max-Planck-Gesellschaft, Leibniz-Gemeinschaft, Fraunhofer-Gesellschaft et cetera), was eine enge Verflechtung zwischen Forschung und Industrie zur Folge hat. Diese intensive Zusammenarbeit zwischen Wirtschaft und Wissenschaft bietet viele Anknüpfungspunkte für Tagungen und Kongresse.

Unsere Vision ist es, gemeinsam mit den Partnern aus Wissenschaft, Wirtschaft und Politik Dresden zu einer der führenden Tagungs- und Kongressstädte Deutschlands zu entwickeln. Vertreter aus Wissenschaft und Forschung zählen mit ihren vielseitigen internationalen Kontakten hierbei zu unseren wichtigsten Botschaftern für den Standort Dresden und das Internationale Congress Center Dresden.

Congress Location

35 Säle bieten Platz für bis zu 6.500 Personen und damit Raum für jede Art von Tagungs- und Kongressveranstaltung.
35 halls offer space for up to 6,500 people and therewith room for all kinds of conference and congress events.

The Dresden region is the most significant growth region in Eastern Germany. It is on its way to develop into one of the most important economic and scientific locations in Germany. Thus, Dresden is always found in a leading position on different economic ranking lists (Prognos Zukunftsatlas, Bellevue Städtetest, Capital-Städterankings). The economy of the city relies on a wide spectrum of industries. The essential growth and development momentum comes from the three future-oriented specialist areas: microelectronics/information and communication technology, nanotechnology/new materials and life sciences/biotechnology. Through the constant build-up and extension of this new sectors, a high density of research institutions has additionally originated (Max Planck Society, Leibniz Association, Fraunhofer Society et cetera), which results in a close interdependence between research and industry. This intensive collaboration between economics and science offers many contact points for conferences and congresses.

It is our vision, together with partners from the scientific, economic and political sectors, to develop Dresden into one of the leading conference and congress cities in Germany. Herewith, representatives from the scientific and research field, with their diversified international contacts, rate among the most important ambassadors for the Dresden location and the International Congress Center Dresden.

Die Semperoper – Ein Leuchtturm in der Dresdner Kulturlandschaft
The Semper Opera House – A beacon in the Dresden cultural landscape

Prof. Gerd Uecker

Der 1946 geborene Autor studierte an der Münchener Musikhochschule Klavier, Musikpädagogik und Dirigieren. Nach Stationen in Köln und Passau wechselte er 1979 an die Staatsoper München, wo er zuletzt Operndirektor war. Seit 2003 ist er Intendant der Semperoper in Dresden. Seit 2005 ist der darüber hinaus Vorsitzender der deutschsprachigen Opernkonferenz.

The author was born in 1946 and studied piano, musical pedagogics and conducting at the Munich University of Music. After stints in Cologne and Passau, he switched to the Munich State Opera in 1979 where his last position was as opera director. He has been the general manager of the Semper Opera House in Dresden since 2003. In 2005, he became the chairman of German Opera Conference.

Dresden definiert sich selbst als eine traditionsreiche Stadt der Kultur und der Künste. Sie tut das selbstbewusst und mit Erfolg. Das Schlagwort von Kultur als „weichem Standortfaktor" gilt hier nicht: Kultur ist für die Landeshauptstadt schon immer das Medium gewesen, aus dem heraus sich die Anziehungskraft und der Ruf des Ortes entwickelt hatte. Handfeste, nachhaltige Beziehungen und Relationen zwischen Kultur und städtischer Infrastruktur, gesellschaftlichem Leben und Attraktivität eines neuen, gewandelten Lebensgefühls haben sich zu einem „starken Faktor" entwickelt, der an diesem Ort Kultur eben nicht nur als Verzierung, Verschönerung oder Ausschmückung eines sonst vom Grau des Erwerbsalltags geprägten Lebens sieht, sondern als etwas Substanzielles, was sich gern als ein spezifisch dresdnerisches Lebenswohlgefühl definiert.

Diese ausgeprägte Verankerung von Kultur in der Tradition Dresdens beeinflusst ihre Entwicklung seit etwa 20 Jahren stark. Fremdenverkehr und Tourismus bescherten nach 1990 einen ungeahnten, boomartigen wirtschaftlichen Aufschwung. Aber auch in dem Bemühen, hochwertige Industriestrukturen durch Ansiedelung großer und bedeutender Firmen zu schaffen, ist das Vorhandensein eines dichten Gewebes lebendiger Kultur ein wesentlicher Faktor. Unternehmen wie VW (Gläserne Manufaktur Dresden) oder der internationale Chiphersteller AMD haben ihre Standortwahl nicht zuletzt auch wegen der lebendigen Kunst- und Kulturszene in Dresden getroffen. Die Technische Universität mit mehr als 35.000 Studenten, das Max-Planck-Institut sowie das Fraunhofer-Institut tragen diese Tatsache mit und runden das Bild ab.

Dresden bietet in der Tat eine im Vergleich mit seiner Einwohnerzahl extrem reiche Szene an Theatern, Museen und einen in seiner Vielfalt schier nicht zu überblickenden, bis ins Kleinste hinein verästelten Konzertbetrieb, durchgängig von Alter Musik bis zum Festival experimenteller zeitgenössischer Musik. Zwei bedeutende, international wirkende und renommierte Symphonieorchester und der weltberühmte Kreuzchor setzen Schwerpunkte im Konzertleben. Daneben gibt es eine Vielzahl kleinerer, qualitativ auf hohem künstlerischem Niveau agierender Ensembles. Die Staatlichen Kunstsammlungen mit dem Grünen Gewölbe im Dresdner Schloss und der Galerie Alte Meister im Zwinger stehen mit der Semperoper im Zentrum des Interesses aller kunstinteressierten Gäste und auch der Dresdner selbst.

Culture

Weltberühmt – Semperoper und Theaterplatz in Dresden.
World famous – The Semper Opera House and the Theaterplatz in Dresden.

Dresden defines itself as a city of culture and art, rich in tradition. The city does this self-confidently and with success. The buzzword of culture as a "soft location factor" does not apply here. For the state capital, culture has always been the medium from which the appeal for and the reputation of the region have developed. Concrete and sustainable connections and relations between culture and city infrastructure, societal life and the attractiveness of a new transformed attitude towards life have developed into a "strong factor", which in this region views culture not only as an adornment, beautification or decoration of the otherwise drab monotony of everyday life, but rather as something substantial, which gladly defines itself as a specific Dresden sense of well-being.

This distinct foothold of culture in the tradition of Dresden has strongly influenced its development for approximately 20 years. An unexpected boom-like economic upswing came about in travel and tourism after 1990. However, also in the effort to create high-quality industrial structures through the settlement of large and distinguished enterprises, the availability of a dense web of lively culture is a significant factor. Organizations such as VW (Transparent Factory Dresden) or the international chip producer AMD, have made their location choice especially also due to the lively art and culture scene in Dresden. The Dresden University of Technology with more than 35,000 students, the Max Planck Institute as well as the Fraunhofer Institute support this fact and round off the picture.

In comparison to its population figure, Dresden in fact offers an extreme abundance of theatres, museums and a branched concert business, which in its diversity is almost not to be overseen. With a concert organization down to the smallest detail, continuing from historic music up to festivals of experimental contemporary music. Two distinguished, internationally active and renowned symphony orchestras and the world-famous Kreuzchor (Choir of the Church of the Holy Cross) place focal points in concert life. In addition, there are numerous smaller ensembles performing at a high level of artistic quality. The Dresden State Art Collections with the Green Vault in the Dresden Castle and the Old Masters Picture Gallery in the Zwinger Palace together with the Semper Opera House form the central interest of all art-loving guests and the people of Dresden themselves.

The Saxon State Opera Dresden counts among the most well-known opera houses in the world. Annually more than 440,000 visitors come to the opera and ballet performances as well as to concerts in the Semper Opera House, which houses an audience of 1,250.

Kultur

Auf mehr als 1.250 Sitzplätzen können in der Semperoper in prachtvollem Ambiente Darbietungen der bekanntesten Interpreten in Opern-, Ballett- und Konzertaufführungen erlebt werden.
In its more than 1,250 seats, performances of the most famous interpreters in ballet, opera and concert can be experienced in a magnificent ambience at the Semper Opera House.

Nach der literarischen Vorlage von Oscar Wilde –
Die Oper Salome von Richard Strauss in einer Inszenierung von Peter Mussbach.
According to Oscar Wilde's literary artwork –
The Salome Opera of Richard Strauss' in a production by Peter Mussbach.

Die Sächsische Staatsoper Dresden zählt zu den bekanntesten Opernhäusern der Welt. Jährlich kommen über 440.000 Besucher zu Opern- und Ballettaufführungen sowie zu Konzerten in die Semperoper, die 1.250 Zuschauern Platz bietet. Weitere 315.000 Besucher lassen sich unter kundiger Führung die Geschichte des Hauses erläutern und bewundern seine erlesene, nach den originalen Plänen Gottfried Sempers rekonstruierte Innenarchitektur.

Das Orchester der Sächsischen Staatsoper ist die international renommierte Sächsische Staatskapelle Dresden, die auch ihre Sinfoniekonzerte, etwa 60 im Jahr, in der Semperoper aufführt sowie daneben den laufenden Opernbetrieb bestreitet. Es ist eines der ältesten Orchester der Welt: Seit ihrer Gründung durch Heinrich Schütz im 16. Jahrhundert besteht und konzertiert sie bis heute ohne zeitliche Unterbrechung.

Der Dresdener Opernbetrieb lässt sich historisch bis in das 17. Jahrhundert hinein zurückverfolgen. Die Dresdner Oper hat Opern- und Musikgeschichte geschrieben. Berühmte Komponisten wirkten hier und gaben den jeweiligen stilistischen Epochen wichtige Impulse: Johann Adolf Hasse der Barockoper, Carl Maria von Weber der deutschen Romantik, Richard Wagner, der als Sachse von Dresden ausgehend in die Operngeschichte des 19. Jahrhunderts wie kein anderer hineingewirkt hat, und Richard Strauss mit seinen revolutionären Uraufführungen von „Salome" und „Elektra" im 20. Jahrhundert.

Heute hat die Sächsische Staatsoper einen höchst lebendigen und produktionsdichten Spielplan: 45 Opern und mehr als zehn Ballettprogramme stehen im Repertoire, über 400 Veranstaltungen pro Jahr in Dresden werden bei einer Gesamtauslastung von etwa 96 Prozent besucht. Im Angebot nehmen Werke von Wolfgang Amadeus Mozart, Richard Wagner und Richard Strauss eine gewichtige Stelle ein. Aber auch die große italienische Oper ist mit vielen Aufführungen vertreten.

Dresden war auch immer schon ein Ort künstlerischer Innovation – so auch im Bereich der Oper. Was wir heute als vertrautes und gesichertes „klassisches" Opernrepertoire ansehen war seinerzeit umstrittene Moderne. Dies gilt sowohl für die Kompositionen von Carl Maria von Weber als auch für die Werke Richard Wagners und natürlich auch von Richard Strauss.

Culture

A further 315,000 visitors are lead through the history of the opera house by expert guided tours and admire its exquisite interior design, which was reconstructed according to the original blueprints of Gottfried Semper.

The orchestra of the Saxon State Opera is the internationally famous Saxon State Orchestra, Dresden, which also performs its about 60 annual symphony concerts at the Semper Opera House as well as additionally dealing with the ongoing opera business. It is one of the oldest orchestras in the world: Since its foundation by Heinrich Schütz in the 16th century, it has existed and given concerts without respite until today.

The Dresden opera establishment historically dates back to the 17th century. The Dresden Opera House has written opera and music history. Famous composers worked here and gave important impetus to the respective stylistic eras: Johann Adolf Hasse, the baroque opera; Carl Maria von Weber, the German romanticism; Richard Wagner, who originated from Dresden in Saxony and affected the history of opera in the 19th century like no other; and Richard Strauss with his revolutionary debut performance of "Salome" and "Elektra" in the 20th century.

Today the Saxon State Opera has an extremely lively and dense production programme: 45 operas and more than ten ballet performances are on the repertoire, over 400 performances are visited annually in Dresden at a total capacity of approximately 96 per cent. In the offered range, the works of Wolfgang Amadeus Mozart, Richard Wagner and Richard Strauss play a prominent role. However, the greatest Italian operas are also represented by numerous performances.

Dresden has also always been a place of artistic innovation – so also in the field of opera. What we today view as the familiar and trusted "classical" opera repertoire, was indisputably modern it its day. This is true as much for the compositions of Carl Maria von Weber as also for the works of Richard Wagner and naturally also those of Richard Strauss. Debut performances at that time, precisely in the era of the legendary conductor Fritz Busch, were seen as a characteristic of the Semper Opera House. Also today, the opera house attempts to continue this tradition incessantly. Herewith the Semper Opera House remains a location of lively debate with contemporary opera, music and aesthetics.

The artistic institutions of Dresden not only stand as representation of a high quality standard – they have fortunately also become a significant economic factor. That is predominantly true with tourism, which constitutes an important earning sector for the city.

Uraufführungen sah man damals, gerade in der Ära des legendären Dirigenten Fritz Busch, als ein Charakteristikum der Semperoper an. Auch heute versucht das Haus diese Tradition ungebrochen fortzusetzen. Die Semperoper bleibt damit ein Ort lebendiger Auseinandersetzung mit zeitgenössischer Oper, Musik und Ästhetik.

Die künstlerischen Institutionen Dresdens stehen nicht nur repräsentativ für einen hohen Qualitätsanspruch, sie sind erfreulicherweise auch zu einem wesentlichen Wirtschaftsfaktor geworden. In erster Linie gilt das im Hinblick auf den Tourismus, der für die Stadt einen wichtigen Erwerbszweig darstellt. Viele Gäste kommen vorrangig des kulturellen Angebots wegen in diese Stadt: Sie buchen Städtereisen, Kultur- und Kunstreisen, besuchen die kulturellen Sehenswürdigkeiten und Highlights Dresdens – und ein Besuch der Semperoper gehört dazu. Vom Billigtourismus der frühen 90er Jahre hat man sich verabschiedet, ein eindeutiger Trend geht heutzutage in Richtung Individual- und inhaltlich anspruchsvoller Gruppenreisen, was sich auch im Dresdner Angebot der Oberklasse-Hotels niederschlägt.

Im Jahre 2007 hat die Semperoper eine Studie durchführen lassen, die die wirtschaftliche Bedeutung des Hauses untersucht hat. Im Ergebnis ließ sich ablesen, dass derzeit etwa 60 Prozent der Besucher der Semperoper von außerhalb kommen (bei einer durchschnittlichen Anreise von 340 Kilometern) und etwa 40 Prozent aus der Region. In dieser Konfiguration schlägt sich ein Rentabilitätsfaktor von 3,9 nieder, der die sogenannte Umwegrentabilität des Hauses darstellt. Mit anderen Worten: Jeder Euro, den der staatliche Träger in die Institution Sächsische Staatsoper Dresden investiert, „rentiert" sich wirtschaftlich mit einem Faktor 3,9 hinsichtlich eines monetären Rückflusses.

Auch was die wirtschaftliche Effizienz des Opernhauses betrifft, steht die Semperoper innerhalb der deutschen Opernhäuser an vorderster Stelle: Der Kostendeckungsgrad, also die Zahl, die angibt, wie viel Prozent der Gesamtausgaben das Opernhaus selbst erwirtschaftet, liegt derzeit bei über 38 Prozent. Angesichts des Bundesdurchschnitts bei deutlich unter 20 Prozent ist dies ein absoluter Spitzenwert.

Dresden und seine reichhaltige Kultur sind mehr als ein Slogan: Es ist ein Lebensgefühl, das eine traditionsreiche Vergangenheit mit einer lebendigen Perspektive in die Zukunft freisinnig verbindet – „Dresden is special".

Richard Wagners „Ring des Nibelungen" in einer Inszenierung von Willy Decker.
Richard Wagner's "Ring des Nibelungen" in a performance by Willy Decker.

Auch mit der Geschichte Dresdens verbunden – Heinrich Schützs „Wie liegt die Stadt so wüste" in einer Produktion von Herbert Wernicke.
Also connected to the history of Dresden – "Wie liegt die Stadt so wüste" by Heinrich Schütz in a production by Herbert Wernicke.

„Giselle" – Der Klassiker des romantischen Handlungsballetts steht seit 160 Jahren auf den Spielplänen großer Bühnen, hier in der Choreographie von David Dawson.
"Giselle" – The classic of romantic ballet d'action has been a part of the repertoire of large arenas for 160 years. According to a choreography by David Dawson on the picture below.

Many visitors come to the city primarily due to the cultural offering in this city: They book city tours, cultural and artistic trips, visit the cultural sights and the highlights of Dresden – and that includes a visit to the Semper Opera House. Cheap tourism of the early nineties has passed – a clear trend these days is towards individual travel and group tours that are demanding as regards content, which is also reflected in the offers of the Dresden upper-class hotels.

In 2007, the Semper Opera House had a survey conducted which investigated the commercial relevance of the opera house. In conclusion, it became visible that at that time about 60 per cent of the Semper Opera House visitors came from outside the region (at an average journey of 340 kilometres) and about 40 per cent from within the region. A profitability factor of 3.9 is reflected in this configuration, which represents the so-called indirect profitability of the opera house. In other words: For every euro the state supporting organization invests in the Saxon State Opera in Dresden, it "profits" commercially at factor 3.9 as regards a monetary backflow. Also as regards the economic efficiency, the Semper Opera House is within the front ranks of the German opera houses: The revenue-to-cost ratio, that is the figure that shows the percentage of total expenditure earned by the opera house itself, currently lies at more than 38 per cent. This is an absolute peak value in view of the national average which lies clearly below 20 per cent.

Dresden and its rich culture are more than a slogan: It is an attitude towards life that liberally combines a past that is rich in tradition with a lively future outlook – "Dresden is special".

Bessere Bedingungen für attraktiven Sport – Dresden bekommt ein neues Stadion
Better conditions for attractive sport – Dresden gets a new stadium

Hauke Haensel

Der 1968 geborenen Autor ist seit 2007 Präsident der SG Dynamo Dresden eV. Nach seinem Studium der Betriebswirtschaftslehre an der Martin Luther Universität Halle-Wittenberg arbeitete er 1992–1997 als Verbandsprüfer beim Sparkassenverband in Berlin. Von 1997–2002 war er Abteilungsleiter Kredit bei der Sparkasse Bernburg und seit 2002 ist er Vorstandsvorsitzender der Volksbank Pirna.

The author was born in 1968 and has been the president of the SG Dynamo Dresden eV since 2007. After his degree in business administration at the Martin Luther Universität Halle-Wittenberg, he worked at the Sparkassenverband in Berlin as an association auditor from 1992–1997. From 1997–2002, he was the head of the credit department at Sparkasse Bernburg, and since 2002, he has been the chairperson of Volksbank Pirna.

Frühjahr 2008. Alle zwei Wochen drängeln sich acht- bis neuntausend Fans im Dresdner Rudolf-Harbig-Stadion, um die Heimspiele Dynamo Dresdens zu erleben. Mancher mag sich in die Nachkriegszeit versetzt fühlen: Das halbe Stadion ist eine Ruine, Trümmerberge und Reste alter Tribünen türmen sich. Der Fantasiebegabte aber kann schon die Umrisse des Neuen erblicken: Betonpfeiler markieren den künftigen Grundriss der Stadionschüssel, erste Treppen und Zugänge sind in Beton gegossen – Dresdens neues Fußballstadion wächst, eine Arena, die 32.000 Zuschauern Platz bietet und die Bedingungen für den Spitzenfußball grundlegend verbessert.

Nach langem, zuweilen zähem „Vorspiel" – erste Überlegungen zum neuen Stadion gab es Mitte der 1990er Jahre – hatte hier seit Herbst 2007 Sportstättenspezialist HBM damit begonnen, in das alte Stadion eine neues zu bauen. Anderthalb Jahre zuvor gaben die Dresdner Stadträte dafür grünes Licht, die Stadt übernahm eine Bürgschaft von rund 40 Millionen Euro, die Planung wurden in vielen öffentlichen Foren diskutiert, der Abriss schließlich begann mit einer Aktion, die erhellte, welchen Stellenwert der Fußball und Dynamo Dresden in Ostsachsen haben. Tausende kamen, um sich Sitzschalen oder Schilder abzubauen – und zahlten dafür oft erkleckliche Summen auf das Konto einer neu errichteten Stiftung, die den Dresdner Nachwuchsfußball fördern hilft.

Tatsächlich hat das Stadion, seit rund 50 Jahren die Heimat Dynamos, Kultstatus. Hier erlebten schon die Großväter und Väter der heute jungen Fans großen Fußball, hier traten in Europacup-Spielen Bayern München, der AS Rom, FC Liverpool oder Benfica Lissabon an. Hierher holten Dynamo-Stars wie Dixi Dörner, Hans-Jürgen Kreische, Ulf Kirsten oder Matthias Sammer DDR-Meistertitel und Pokale.

Sports

Animation des im Bau befindlichen neuen Stadions.
Animation of the new stadium with construction still in progress.

© beyer architekten

Spring 2008. Every two weeks, eight to nine thousand fans swarm to the Dresden Rudolf-Harbig Stadium to watch the home games of Dynamo Dresden. Some may feel themselves displaced to the post-war period: Half the stadium is in ruins, mounds of debris and the remains of old grandstands are piled up. However, those with imagination can already catch a glimpse of the silhouette of the new stadium. Concrete columns mark the future floor plan of the stadium bowl, the first steps and entrances are cast in concrete – Dresden's new football stadium is growing, an arena that offers seats for 32,000 spectators and fundamentally improves the conditions for first-class football.

After long, sometimes tough "foreplay" – the first considerations for a stadium started in the mid 1990s – the sports facilities specialist HBM started building a new stadium in the old stadium here in autumn 2007. One and a half years earlier, the Dresden city councils gave the green light for it, the city took a guarantee for more than 40 million euros, the planning was debated in many public forums, the demolition finally began with an activity which shed light on the significance of football and Dynamo Dresden in East Saxony: Thousands came to remove the seat buckets or shields – and often paid considerable amounts into the bank account of a newly established foundation which helps promote youth football in Dresden.

The stadium, which has been the home of Dynamo for about 50 years, has in actual fact got cult status. Here, the grandfathers and fathers of the young fans today already experienced great football; here Bayern München, AS Rom, FC Liverpool and Benfica Lisbon competed in the Europe Cup Games. Here, Dynamo stars such as Dixi Dörner, Hans-Jürgen Kreische, Ulf Kirsten or Matthias Sammer got GDR master titles and cups; national league football was shown in this stadium after 1990 until the economic crash of Dynamo in the mid 1990s; here the cumbersome rebuilding and the acclaimed comeback into the second league and finally the mourning of the renewed descent into the third league took place. The up and down sways of Dynamo Dresden since the reunification have numerous causes – one undoubtedly lies therein that the economic general conditions for professional sports, particularly for the national and even international football, in the East of Germany have only slowly been developing and currently still noticeably lag behind those of the old federal states.

Neue Ränge in Beton für 32.000 Zuschauer.
New concrete tiers for 32,000 spectators.

In diesem Stadion gab es nach 1990 bis zum wirtschaftlichen Crash Dynamos Mitte der 90er Jahre Bundesliga-Fußball zu sehen, hier vollzogen sich der mühsame Neuaufbau und der bejubelte Wiederaufstieg in die zweite Liga, und hier wurde schließlich der erneute Abstieg in die Regionalliga betrauert.

Das Auf und Ab Dynamo Dresdens seit der Wiedervereinigung hat viele Gründe – einer liegt zweifellos darin, dass sich die wirtschaftlichen Rahmenbedingungen für den Profisport, insbesondere für den nationalen oder gar internationalen Fußball, im Osten Deutschlands nur langsam entwickeln und derzeit noch immer spürbar hinter denen in den alten Bundesländern zurückbleiben.

Dresden und seine Region gehören zu den dynamischsten Wirtschaftsstandorten im Osten, die Landeshauptstadt ist mittlerweile ein Zentrum der Mikroelektronik von europäischem Rang, sie genießt einen guten Ruf als Kultur- und Wissenschaftsmetropole, kann noch immer auf gute Kerne der feinmechanischen Industrie, des Geräte- und des Maschinenbaus verweisen, der VW-Konzern produziert in Dresden seine Luxus-Limousinen. Doch die Wirtschaftsstruktur der Stadt und ihres Umfeldes ist vor allem von kleinen und mittleren Unternehmen geprägt, zu denen erfreulicherweise viele aus dem forschungsnahen Bereich gespeiste Neugründungen kommen.

Das spiegelt sich auch wider in der Zusammensetzung der Sponsoren Dynamos:

Sports

Das neue Stadion wächst.
The new stadium is developing.

Dresden and its region belong to the most dynamic economic locations in the East, the state capital is meanwhile a centre of microelectronics of European standing; it enjoys a good reputation as a cultural and scientific metropolis; it can still refer to good core industries such as the fine mechanical industry and tool and machine building industry; the VW Group produces their luxury limousines in Dresden. But the economic structure of the city and its surroundings is shaped primarily by small and medium-sized enterprises, added to which are fortunately many newly-founded organizations supported by the research-related sector.

This is reflected in the composition of the sponsors of Dynamo: Many small and medium-sized, mostly owner-managed enterprises involve themselves with tremendous dedication. Major sponsors seldom make an appearance, and if they do, it will be because of the commitment of organizations that in a particular manner find themselves personally connected to the development in the East. The international marketing chain, on the other hand, only in a few exceptional cases reaches as far as Dresden football.

In this situation, the building of a new, attractive stadium may be regarded as an opportunity to open doors and to improve the economic survival conditions of a club which can refer to great traditions, a both large and committed following and deep roots in its home region.

Sitzschalen: begehrte Andenken bei Jung und Alt.
Seat buckets: a popular keepsake for young and old.

Spitzenfußball braucht eine kontinuierliche gute Nachwuchsarbeit.
First-class football requires a constant flow of youth development work.

Mit großer Opferbereitschaft engagieren sich viele kleine und mittlere, meist inhabergeführte Unternehmen. Großsponsoren treten selten in Erscheinung und wenn, dann dank des Engagements von Unternehmern, die sich in besonderer Weise der Entwicklung im Osten Deutschlands persönlich verbunden fühlen. Die internationale Vermarktungskette hingegen reicht nur in wenigen Ausnahmen bis zum Dresdner Fußball.

In dieser Situation darf der Bau eines neuen, attraktiven Stadions als Chance angesehen werden, Türen zu öffnen und die wirtschaftlichen Existenzbedingungen eines Vereins zu verbessern, der auf große Traditionen, eine ebenso große wie engagierte Fangemeinde und eine tiefe Verwurzelung in seiner Heimatregion verweisen kann.

Die neue Dresdner Arena verfügt über alles, was im Profi-Fußball heute als unerlässlich gilt, um oben „mitzuspielen": gut ausgebaute, sichere Ränge, überhaupt bessere Möglichkeiten, um Sicherheit und Ordnung im Stadion zu gewährleisten, vergleichsweise viel Parkraum auf dem Stadion-Gelände und hervorragende Trainings- und Wettkampf-Bedingungen für die Spieler, beste Arbeitsmöglichkeiten für die Medien – und vor allem auch ein breites Angebot für Sponsoren.

Neben 22 VIP-Logen gibt es einen gut ausgestatteten variablen Bereich, der Sponsoren und anderen Interessenten nicht allein während der Spiele zur Verfügung steht, sondern auch für Marketing-Events, Betriebsfeste, kleine Kongresse oder Ausstellungs- wie Verkaufsveranstaltungen. Das Interesse daran wie an den Logen ist groß und zeigt, auf welche Potenziale die Stadion-Betreiber und die Geschäftsführung des Vereins künftig zurückgreifen können. Dazu gehört auch die Möglichkeit, im Stadion Konzerte und andere Großveranstaltungen durchzuführen. Alles in allem ist Dynamo Dresden künftig aufgerufen, neue Ideen zu entwickeln, um sein neues „Heim" nicht nur besser auszulasten, sondern zu einem wirklichen Zentrum des Vereinslebens zu machen.

Bei allen Chancen, die ein modernes Stadion bietet – sie können nur effektiv genutzt werden, wenn sich der sportliche Erfolg einstellt. Dafür sind nicht allein wirtschaftliche Umfeld-Faktoren ausschlaggebend. Spitzenfußball braucht auch eine kontinuierlich gute Nachwuchsarbeit. Dynamo Dresden kann dabei auf gute Voraussetzungen zurückgreifen, die die Stadt Dresden mit einem neuen Sportschul-Zentrum geschaffen hat. In dessen unmittelbarer Nähe befinden sich Internats- und Arbeitsräume des Nachwuchsleistungszentrums des Vereins – geschaffen mit Hilfe der Ulf Kirsten-Stiftung und vieler weiterer Spender. Der Verein bringt für den Betrieb dieses Zentrums Jahr für Jahr erhebliche Summen auf. Wir sind davon überzeugt, dass dies eine Investition ist, die, wie auch das neue Stadion, die Zukunft des Dresdner Fußballs und die von Dynamo Dresden sichert.

The new Dresden arena possesses everything that is regarded as essential to play in the upper leagues in professional football: well developed, safe tiers, even better possibilities to guarantee security and orderliness in the stadium, comparably many parking spaces on the stadium premises and excellent training and match conditions for the players, the best employment opportunities for the media – and above all, also a wide selection for sponsors.

In addition to 22 VIP boxes, there is a well-equipped variable section, which is available to sponsors and interested parties not only during matches but also for marketing events, company functions, small congresses or exhibitions as well as sales activities. The interest shown in it as also in the boxes is great and shows what potential the stadium operators and the club management can fall back on in the future. Additionally, there is also the possibility of holding concerts and other large events in the stadium. All in all, Dynamo Dresden is in future called upon to develop new ideas to not only better use its new "home" to its full capacity, but rather to make it into a real centre of club activities.

For all the prospects that a modern stadium has to offer – it can only be effectively utilized if the sporting success materializes. Business environment factors alone cannot be decisive. First-class football also requires a constant flow of youth development work. Dynamo Dresden can thereby draw on good preconditions, which the city of Dresden has created with a new sports college centre. Within its immediate vicinity, boarding schools and work groups of the club's youth development centre are situated – created with the help of the Ulf Kirsten Foundation and numerous other sponsors. Year after year, the club gets together significant amounts of money for the operation of this centre. We are convinced that this investment, as well as the new stadium, safeguards the future of football in Dresden and that of Dynamo Dresden.

Fakten

Bevölkerung
im Direktionsbezirk Dresden (Stand: 01.01.2008)

insgesamt	1.646.716
Fläche in qkm	7.931,10
Eheschließungen (2007)	6.905
Geburten (2007)	14.060
Geburten-/Sterbesaldo	– 4.007
Bevölkerungszunahme	3.151
Haushalte	859.700

Fläche

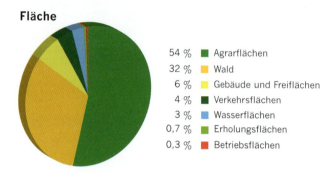

- 54 % Agrarflächen
- 32 % Wald
- 6 % Gebäude und Freiflächen
- 4 % Verkehrsflächen
- 3 % Wasserflächen
- 0,7 % Erholungsflächen
- 0,3 % Betriebsflächen

Gesamtfläche: 793.098 Hektar

Wirtschaft
(im Direktionsbezirk Dresden)

Bruttoinlandsprodukt (in Milliarden Euro)	30,5
BIP-Entwicklung 2000–2006	+ 20 %
Erwerbstätige (2006)	751.800
Arbeitslose (2007)	122.538

Wirtschaftszweige *(im Direktionsbezirk Dresden)*	Beschäftigte
Landwirtschaft, Forst, Fischerei	10.940
Verarbeitendes Gewerbe	112.794
Baugewerbe	37.668
Bergbau, Gewinnung von Steinen und Erden	6.954
Handel, Instandhaltung und Reparatur von Kraftfahrzeugen und Gebrauchsgütern	64.182
Gastgewerbe	19.514
Verkehr und Nachrichtenübermittlung	29.680
Kredit- und Versicherungsgewerbe	10.493
Grundstücks- und Wohnungswesen, Vermietung	72.487
Erbringung von wirtschaftlichen Dienstleistungen	134.031
Öffentliche Verwaltung, sonstige öff. und priv. Verwaltung	41.687

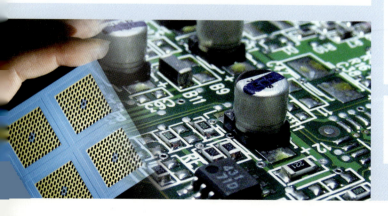

Das besondere Extra

Die Region Dresden zeichnet sich wesentlich durch drei echte Alleinstellungsmerkmale aus – Forschung, Kultur und Internationalität:
1. Dresden ist mit 18 außeruniversitären Instituten der drei renommiertesten Forschungsgesellschaften der forschungsintensivste Standort Deutschlands.
2. Die Region hat mit dem Dresdner Barock-Ensemble, der Semperoper und der Frauenkirche als wichtigstem Symbol des gesamtdeutschen Wiederaufbaus sowie mit dem Elbsandsteingebirge weltbekannte kulturelle und touristische Höhepunkte und zeichnet sich durch eine hohe Lebensqualität aus.
3. Die Grenznähe zu Polen und Tschechien wird von der heimischen Wirtschaft für den internationalen Austausch vorteilhaft genutzt.

Standort auf einen Blick
The location at a glance

Verkehrsanbindung

Internationaler Flughafen Dresden	1.854.378 Fluggäste
Straßen (inkl. Autobahnen)	5.749.477 km
ICE-Bahnhof Dresden	
Hafen Dresden-Friedrichstadt	42 Hektar (20 Liegeplätze)

Kultur

Die Staatlichen Kunstsammlungen Dresden tragen die berühmtesten staatlichen Museen der Stadt Dresden. Schloss und Zwinger sind die zentralen Einrichtungen für die Gemäldegalerien Alte Meister (unter anderem Raffael, Rembrandt, Rubens, Canaletto) und Neue Meister (unter anderem Caspar David Friedrich, Max Liebermann, Slevogt, Dix und Künstler der „Brücke").

Tourismus 2007

Angebotene Bettenplätze	56.580
Gästeübernachtungen	7.999.123

Wissenschaft und Forschung

11	Hochschulen, *allein an der TU Dresden werden 35.000 Studenten ausgebildet*
5	Institute/Zentren der Leibniz-Gemeinschaft
3	Institute der Max-Planck-Gesellschaft
10	Institute/Zentren der Fraunhofer-Gesellschaft

Kaufwerte für Bauland 2007	Euro/qm
baureifes Land	74,56
Rohbauland	6,94
sonstiges Bauland	7,74

Facts

That special extra

The Dresden region distinguishes itself through three genuine unique selling points – research, culture and internationality:
1. With 18 non-university institutions of the three most prestigious research societies, Dresden is the most research-intensive location in Germany.
2. With the Dresden Baroque Ensemble, the Semper Opera and the Frauenkirche as the most important symbol of the all-German reconstruction, as well as the Elbe Sandstone Mountains, the region has world-renowned cultural and tourism highlights and distinguishes itself by a high quality of life.
3. The close proximity to the Polish and Czech borders is favourably used for international exchange by the domestic economy.

Transport connection

Dresden International Airport	1,854,378 passengers
Roads (incl. motorways)	5,749,477 km
Dresden ICE Railway Station	
Dresden-Friedrichstadt Harbour	42 hectares (20 mooring berths)

Culture

The Dresden State Art Collections carry the most famous state museums of the city of Dresden. The Schloss (palace) and Zwinger (dungeon) are the central installations for the Old Masters Picture Gallery (amongst others Raffael, Rembrandt, Rubens, Canaletto) and the New Masters Gallery (amongst others Caspar David Friedrich, Max Liebermann, Slevogt, Dix and artists of the "The Bridge").

Tourism 2007

Offered beds	56,580
Overnight guests	7,999,123

Science & research

11	Universities, 35,000 students are educated at the TU Dresden alone
5	Institutes/Centres of the Leibniz Association
3	Institutes of the Max Planck Society
10	Institutes/Centres of the Fraunhofer Society

Market values for building land 2007	euros/m²
ready-for-building land	74.56
unprepared building land	6.94
other building land	7.74

Population
in the Dresden Administrative Region (Status: 01.01.2008)

Overall	1,646,716
Area in km²	7,931.10
Marriages (2007)	6,905
Births (2007)	14,060
Birth-/death balance	– 4,007
Population increase	3,151
Households	859,700

Area distribution

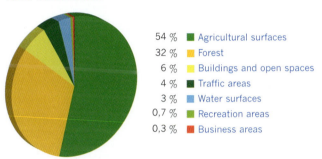

- 54 % Agricultural surfaces
- 32 % Forest
- 6 % Buildings and open spaces
- 4 % Traffic areas
- 3 % Water surfaces
- 0,7 % Recreation areas
- 0,3 % Business areas

Total area: 793,098 hectares

Economy
(in the Dresden Administrative Region)

Gross domestic product (in billion euros)	30.5
GDP growth 2000–2006	+ 20 %
Gainfully employed persons (2006)	751,800
Unemployed persons (2007)	122,538

Economic sectors	Workforce
(in the Dresden Administrative Region)	
Agriculture, Forestry, Fishing	10,940
Manufacturing	112,794
Construction	37,668
Mining, extraction of non-metallic minerals	6,954
Trade, maintenance and repair of motor vehicles and consumer goods	64,182
Hotel and restaurant industry	19,514
Communication and information transmission	29,680
Credit and insurance industry	10,493
Real estate and housing, tenancy	72,487
Provision of commercial services	134,031
Public administration, other private and public administration	41,687

Unternehmensverzeichnis

ADZ Nagano GmbH
Bergener Ring 43
D-01458 Ottendorf-Okrilla
Telefon +49 (0) 35205 5969-30
Telefax +49 (0) 35205 5969-59
www.adz.de
S. 65

**BA
Berufsakademie Sachsen**
Heideparkstraße 8
D-01099 Dresden
Telefon +49 (0) 351 81334-0
Telefax +49 (0) 351 81334-29
www.ba-dresden.de
S. 38

Dresden International University gGmbH
Chemnitzer Straße 46b
D-01187 Dresden
Telefon +49 (0) 351 463-32326
Telefax +49 (0) 351 463-33956
www.dresden-international-university.de
S. 39

**Europäische Forschungsgesellschaft
Dünne Schichten eV**
Gostritzer Straße 63
D-01217 Dresden
Telefon +49 (0) 351 8718-370
Telefax +49 (0) 351 8718-431
www.efds.org
S. 72

**Fraunhofer-Institut für
Werkstoff- und Strahltechnik IWS**
Winterbergstraße 28
D-01277 Dresden
Telefon +49 (0) 351 2583-324
Telefax +49 (0) 351 2583-300
www.iws.fraunhofer.de
S. 48

**Fraunhofer-Institut
für Elektronenstrahl- und Plasmatechnik**
Winterbergstraße 28
D-01277 Dresden
Telefon +49 (0) 351 2586-0
Telefax +49 (0) 351 2586-105
www.fep.fraunhofer.de
S. 49

**Glatt Systemtechnik GmbH
Dresden (GST)**
Grunaer Weg 26
D-01277 Dresden
Telefon +49 (0) 351 2584-325
Telefax +49 (0) 351 2584-328
www.glatt.com
S. 64

**GebäudeEnsemble
Deutsche Werkstätten
Grundbesitz Hellerau GmbH**
Moritzburger Weg 67
D-01109 Dresden
Telefon +49 (0) 351 8838-201
Telefax +49 (0) 351 8838-245
www.hellerau-gb.de   S. 96

**HTI
Dinger & Hortmann KG**
Dresdner Straße 2
D-01665 Klipphausen
Telefon +49 (0) 35204 966-0
Telefax +49 (0) 35204 966-38
www.hti-dinger-hortmann.de   S. 83

Leybold Optics Dresden GmbH
Zur Wetterwarte 50/Haus 303
D-01109 Dresden
Telefon +49 (0) 351 86695-16
Telefax +49 (0) 351 86695-17
www.leyboldoptics.com   S. 82

**Max-Planck-Institut für
Chemische Physik fester Stoffe**
Nöthnitzer Straße 40
D-01187 Dresden
Telefon +49 (0) 351 4646-3602
Telefax +49 (0) 351 4646-10
www.cpfs.mpg.de   S. 56

**Max-Planck-Institut
für Physik komplexer Systeme**
Nöthnitzer Straße 38
D-01187 Dresden
Telefon +49 (0) 351 871-0
Telefax +49 (0) 351 871-1999
www.pks.mpg.de   S. 57

**Nehlsen-BWB Flugzeug-Galvanik Dresden
GmbH & Co. KG**
Grenzstraße 2
D-01109 Dresden
Telefon +49 (0) 351 8831-400
Telefax +49 (0) 351 8831-404
www.flugzeuggalvanik.de   S. 26

**Schiffs- und Yachtwerft
Dresden GmbH**
Österreicher Straße 95
D-01279 Dresden
Telefon +49 (0) 351 21111-70
Telefax +49 (0) 351 21111-99
www.sywdresden.de   S. 97

Spezialtechnik Dresden GmbH
Zum Windkanal 21
D-01109 Dresden
Telefon +49 (0) 351 886-5000
Telefax +49 (0) 351 886-5443
www.spezialtechnik.de   S. 27

Wirtschafts- und Wissenschaftsstandort Region Dresden
Business and Science Location of the Dresden Region

EUROPÄISCHER WIRTSCHAFTS VERLAG GmbH
Ein Unternehmen der MEDIEN GRUPPE KIRK AG
Hilpertstraße 1 in D-64295 Darmstadt
Telefon +49 (0) 6151 1770-0
Telefax +49 (0) 6151 1770-20
ewv@ebn24.com
www.ebn24.com

Verlag/Publishing House

Christian Kirk ©
in Zusammenarbeit mit dem Freistaat Sachsen und der Region Dresden

Herausgeber/Publisher

Dieses Projekt wurde realisiert unter Mitarbeit der Autoren
Stanislaw Tillich, Thomas Jurk, Dr. habil. Henry Hasenpflug,
Dr. Michael Hupe, Dr. Detlef Hamann, Klaus Wurpts, Dr. Eva-Maria Stange,
Ulrich Assmann, Prof. Dr. Eckhard Beyer, Prof. Dr. Kai Simons,
Prof. Dr. Peter Kücher, Andreas Huhn, Prof. Dr.-Ing. Dieter Weidlich,
Markus H. Michalow, Dr. Wilhelm W. Zörgiebel, Gerhard Riegger,
Prof. Gerd Uecker, Hauke Haensel
sowie in der Organisation
Andreas Laue, Harald Thoebes, Melanie Kirk-Becker

Realisation

MEDIA TEAM Gesellschaft für Kommunikation mbH
Bernhard Knapstein (Chefredakteur),
Magdalena Noffke, Röbke Wulff
und Christine Schuster (Schlussredaktion)

Gesamtherstellung/Collect-run Production
Redaktion/Editorial stuff

Katharina Jedral-Tomski, Achim Kunz, Irina Neugum,
Stina Pfaff, Mareike Stahl und Christian Trott

Grafik & Satz/Graphics & Typesetting

Lesley-Ann Knoll

Übersetzung/Translation

Autoren der Artikel, porträtierte Unternehmen,
© Flughafen Dresden GmbH / Weimer; © Gerd Kleiner/PIXELIO; © Matthias Creutziger;
© Peter Wiegel/PIXELIO; © Renate-Franke/PIXELIO; © RENEUM/PIXELIO;
© S. Hofschläger/PIXELIO; Abbildung: Koenig & Bauer AG; GWT-TUD GmbH;
Infineon Technologies AG; www.sachsen.de

Bildnachweis/Picture credits

gedruckt bei abcdruck in Heidelberg auf Heidelberger Speedmaster,
auf 100 Prozent chlorfreiem Papier

Druck/Print

Alle Rechte vorbehalten. Kein Teil dieses Buches darf ohne schriftliche Genehmigung
des Verlages vervielfältigt oder verarbeitet werden. Unter dieses Verbot fällt insbesondere
die gewerbliche Vervielfältigung per Kopie, die Aufnahme ins Internet oder andere
elektronische Datenbanken und die Vervielfältigung auf CD.
Verstöße werden rechtlich verfolgt.
Redaktionsschluss: 15. Mai 2009

Vervielfältigung & Nachdruck/ Reproduction & Reprints

978-3-938630-65-5, Ausgabe 2009/2010

ISBN